Obsessive Compulsive Disorder

The Ultimate Guide to Taking Back Your Life

(How to Free Yourself From Obsessive Compulsive Disorder)

Wayne Baxter

Published By **John Kembrey**

Wayne Baxter

Obsessive Compulsive Disorder: The Ultimate Guide to Taking Back Your Life (How to Free Yourself From Obsessive Compulsive Disorder)

ISBN   978-1-998038-11-4

Legal & Disclaimer

Table Of Contents

Chapter 1: Define And Symptoms Of Ocd

Are you constantly thinking about something you don't want to think about? Do you find yourself repeating actions without feeling helpless to stop? Then it could be that you suffer from OCD. In this chapter, I will define what OCD is and discuss its symptoms in greater detail.

What Is OCD?

OCD, also known as obsessive-compulsive disorder, is a psychological condition that causes unwanted feelings and thoughts (obsessions). You may also feel the urge to do something repeatedly (compulsion), even if you don't want to. Some OCD sufferers experience only compulsions, some only obsessions, while others possess both traits simultaneously.

People suffering from OCD know their feelings and thoughts have no value; it is something they dislike, yet they have no control over it. Quitting seems impossible and often leads them to repeat things against their will; when they finally do stop, the feeling of relief is temporary; soon afterwards they begin again to repeat unwanted activities.

Repetitive thoughts or habits are something everyone experiences at some point in their life. However, when these actions and thoughts start interfering with social life, job, or any other area of one's life - then it could be classified as OCD. *You have no control over them even if you wish for control - even when trying!

* Take up a lot of your time.

Symptoms of OCD

OCD typically presents with one or both symptoms. At first, these may seem like harmless behaviors but when something negative happens such as death of a loved one, abuse, or any personal crisis, those compulsions and obsessions may become overwhelming. Obsessions: these could include thoughts of the future that don't make sense and lead to physical and psychological suffering. Compulsions: Focusing on something despite having other commitments (like work). Obsessions: Excesses occur when something important gets put off; obsessions: these urges cause anxiety/happiness/fearfulness/tease: obsessions

An obsession is a fear or uncontrollable thought that causes stress. Examples of obsessional thinking include: * Suspicion that your partner may be deceiving you even when there is no evidence to back this up

* You are constantly aware of breathing, blinking eyes and other body sensations.

* You experience intense worry - either for others or yourself.

* You feel nervous using public washrooms, touching doorknobs or shaking hands with others.

Signs That You Have Obsessive Thoughts

* You fear germs and dirt. Your fear of getting dirty may lead to touching objects like doorknobs or individuals who have touched these items that you consider "filthy." You may even avoid shaking hands with others or hugging them if there is any physical contact between the two of you.

* You feel an overwhelming need to maintain order. You become so obsessed with getting everything in its proper place that it becomes an obsession, exhausting yourself in pursuit of perfection. When something seems out of whack, however, you become so stressed that other tasks become unmanageable until everything is back to its original state of calm.

* You experience intense fear of harming someone or yourself. Even if the thought is

completely different, suddenly you start thinking about harming yourself or someone else. Imagine walking on a sunny and fun day and suddenly having thoughts of getting involved in an accident or falling somewhere along the path; no matter how hard you try not to think about that part, it always creeps up on you.

* You feel overwhelmed and uncertain when making mistakes. It can be easy to become fearful or doubtful when other people don't reassure you that what you are doing is right or correct; but if someone keeps telling you yes, that makes things a little better; however, if other people don't reassure you, your fear of making errors increases and eventually leads to panicky behaviour which ultimately results in making errors yourself.

* You fear being embarrassed. Are you worried that you won't fit in with the crowd or say something stupid or inappropriate. Doing so causes you to avoid serious or

intense conversations out of fear of appearing foolish or incorrect, leading you to become self-conscious in front of others while endangerling yourself in the process?
* Are you trying so hard to protect yourself that it ends up embarrassing yourself instead

* You struggle with hostile and negative thoughts. These could include distorted ideas about religion or sexuality that you find offensive, yet cannot seem to stop invading your mind. Whether it's an upsetting situation at work or home, the thought can be unbearably distressing; whatever the case, these experiences often leave you with lasting emotional scars that make life difficult.

Compulsions

If you find yourself repeatedly repeating an action or ritual, that can be classified as a compulsion. Some examples of compulsive behaviour: * Always wanting to count things like bottles and footsteps

* You repeat a task until you feel that you have accomplished it the desired number of times.

Symptoms of compulsive behaviour

You find it impossible to stop cleaning or washing. Do you find yourself repeatedly handwashing, taking baths repeatedly, or wiping objects several times? Have your hands become so dry that the skin becomes raw and cracked? These behaviors could indicate an underlying compulsion.

You just can't seem to stop checking. Even after doing something as mundane as locking your doors and going outside, you find yourself checking them 6-7 more times even though you know for certain it has been verified. It becomes an obsession.

* Another example is when you've just finished cooking and are trying to pack up.

But before leaving your kitchen, you keep checking whether all appliances have been turned off, the refrigerator door closed properly, or whether the chimney light had been turned off altogether. Before going to bed that night, you double-check whether all lights in your bathroom have been turned off properly.

* You find yourself counting out loud your numbers.

* You want everything organized: you eat certain food in a particular order; organize items in your kitchen cupboard or closet according to a certain system.

* If there's something that needs fixing, you can become anxious. Your top priority becomes getting that item back into order - no matter how urgent other tasks may be. No matter how urgent other tasks may be, you will put off getting everything "right" until everything is in its proper place.

* You place great importance on routines. Doing or saying things the same way for multiple times will become second nature to you, and only then will you feel free to leave home.

* You find yourself hoarding or collecting. Despite having many unnecessary possessions in your house that you never use, it seems impossible to stop yourself from buying more of them.

* Imagine having enough clothes and shoes, yet still finding yourself drawn to shopping even though your wardrobe is overflowing!

Symptoms of OCD in Children

Early signs of OCD can begin during adolescence or even childhood. Common symptoms associated with this disorder in children include: * Difficulty maintaining relationships and friendships

* The child suffered physical illness as a result of stress.

Chapter 2: Causes Of Ocd

Obsessive-Compulsive disorder, also known as OCD or Obsessive-Honeymoon disorder, is a mental condition in which individuals experience repetitive unwanted sensations or thoughts (obsessions) or the urge to do something repeatedly (compulsions).

Some OCD patients only experience obsessions, others only compulsions and still others have both symptoms.

Someone with OCD may experience obsessive thoughts which lead to compulsive behaviors. As a result, they may repeat something over and over until they believe it has been completed enough times.

Some individuals become compulsive over checking if they've turned off all the lights, appliances, touched anything filthy and/or locked the doors before leaving their home. But this kind of attention to detail doesn't always fill those with OCD feelings;

oftentimes these tasks seem mundane to those without OCD.

They know it is foolish and pointless, yet they cannot stop themselves from engaging in compulsive behaviors. It's like they understand that what they're doing is unhealthy, yet feel powerless to stop. In this chapter, I will examine some possible causes that may contribute to OCD.

What Causes Obsessive-Compulsive Disorder?

The exact cause of OCD remains a mystery, as patients try to uncover what triggers it. Some OCD patients tend to be over thinkers, believing that by uncovering the source of their condition they might be able to effectively address it and find relief. But this belief can be misguided: uncovering its origin could potentially provide relief and allow patients to move on with their lives.

Many patients struggle to comprehend the source of their OCD. Some report it was triggered by something in their life such as doubtful interactions, cannabis use or traumatizing experiences. Well, it's true that some past events can trigger symptoms in people - this has even been observed across cultures through cross-cultural OCD studies.

Research is ongoing to understand what causes OCD. While no single theory can fully account for every individual's experience, researchers believe certain elements are likely involved in inducing it: * Personality * Personal Experiences * Biological Factors* Unstoppable Impulses * Serotonin System

* Genetics

* Cognitive-Behavioral Theories.

* Psychodynamic Theories*

Personality

Studies have suggested that individuals with certain personality traits are more prone to developing OCD. If you're methodical, meticulous or have high standards, research suggests you could be at greater risk for this disorder.

Personal Experiences

Studies have also indicated a correlation between certain personality traits and personal experiences.

Studies have indicated that OCD may be caused by certain personal experiences in one's past life. Examples include:

Your childhood experiences of abuse, bullying, violence or trauma may have contributed to the development of OCD in you. These compulsions and obsessions could have developed as defensive mechanisms against all the anxiety caused by these circumstances.

Maybe your parents did the same thing. If both of your parents suffered from anxiety issues, you may have picked up on their compulsive behaviors as coping methods.

There may be an on-going stress or concern in your life. If you are going through stressful events like joining a new occupation or being injured, this could be the triggering incident for OCD, or it could aggravate existing symptoms.

Some may experience OCD as a result of pregnancy. When embarking on a new journey or facing major changes in one's life, such as adding additional responsibilities soon after birth, OCD can often arise.

Biological Factors

According to certain biological theories, when your mind lacks serotonin, it could play an important role in producing OCD. However, it remains uncertain if this causes OCD or simply contributes to it.

Research is ongoing to discover how various parts of the mind might contribute to OCD, but no definitive answers have yet been identified.

Studies on the biological causes of OCD involve research into the circuit relay system that exists between the orbitofrontal cortex and thalamus.

The orbitofrontal cortex is responsible for all your complex behaviors, such as reward-based decision-making, assessment, emotional regulation and goal-directed behavior.

The orbitofrontal cortex' loop circuits branch off to other regions like the basal ganglia's caudate nucleus. This area plays a role in processing voluntary motor movements and cognition.

Once these circuits are activated, your attention is drawn to these impulses and you act upon them by engaging in a specific behavior that directly addresses the impulse.

Consider this scenario: you have just used the toilet and are now washing your hands to eliminate all germs on them. Once you finish washing (the appropriate behaviour for that impulse), your brain circuit diminishes, so you stop cleaning your hands and carry on with your day as normal.

Unstoppable Impulses

When you have OCD, certain impulses in the brain cannot be ignored or suppressed. Therefore, you may experience compulsive behaviors and obsessions as well as uncontrollable thoughts.

Consider what happens if your brain cannot stop thinking about germs on your hands, leading you to repeatedly wash them.

Compulsions and obsessions may be connected to contamination, aggressiveness and sexuality; your brain circuit plays a role in controlling these things as well.

Neuroimaging studies have confirmed abnormal activities within this circuitry.

Serotonin System

Some OCD patients respond to treatments such as selective serotonin reuptake inhibitors (SSRIs).

They may be responsible for stimulating neurochemical serotonin, suggesting that any issues with brain circuits could potentially have an underlying connection with the serotonin system.

Genetics

Some believe that OCD may have a genetic component. If you have family members suffering from OCD, there is an increased chance for you to develop it as well; around 25% of individuals diagnosed with OCD have either relatives or parents who also suffer from it.

Studies have revealed that twins who share an OCD diagnosis can develop it too. Genetics plays a significant role, with research suggesting there are 30% to 50% chances of your child developing OCD as a result of genetics alone.

Cognitive-Behavioural Theories

All of us experience unexpected or bizarre thoughts throughout the day. Cognitive-behavioural theories of OCD suggest that if you are prone to OCD, then these strange feelings cannot be ignored.

Additionally, those suffering from OCD may feel the need to control their thoughts in order to protect themselves. They might worry that they are going insane due to these unexpected and unexplained thoughts; additionally, they may fear realizing these feelings (such as hurting loved ones) are true.

Once you identify these thoughts as dangerous, you become increasingly alert and vigilant. You might check to see if there's a thief in your neighborhood before leaving home for work each day.

Once you start having these thoughts repeatedly, the potential danger increases. A vicious cycle is created and it becomes almost impossible to break free from these anxious feelings; eventually they may lead to obsessions.

Hand washing could be a learned behavior. When you feel infected and stressed out, washing your hands may reduce this unease and leave you with a sense of calmness and comfort.

Thus, this reinforces the behavior of hand washing in an effort to reduce anxiety. When faced with an obsession, or fear of contamination, one may become compulsive in their attempts to soothe their nervousness by repeatedly washing their hands.

Psychodynamic Theories

According to psychodynamic approaches of OCD, compulsions and obsessions could be signs of unconscious conflict. This suggests you may have attempted to manage, resolve or delete something for a prolonged period of time.

Conflicts arise most often when one disagrees with societal norms, that is, when their thoughts or desires are deemed inappropriate by society.

These conflicts might stem from aggression or some sort of sexual drive. When these become overwhelming and unpleasant, the only way to manage them is by transferring them onto something more manageable such as organizing, monitoring, or hand washing tasks.

Psychodynamic treatment procedures suggest that by making patients aware of these conflicts, it could potentially reduce OCD symptoms. Unfortunately, there is still no conclusive evidence to back this up.

Inclined to Obsess

People who have experienced stressful life events in their past often develop symmetrical and checking compulsions after developing OCD symptoms.

They can do it to attempt to maintain some sense of order in an increasingly unpredictable world. While it may be tempting to uncover the underlying cause of OCD, understanding its root cause may not always be possible.

OCD is not caused by late grooming, culture or religion; rather, it's the result of a complex interplay of stressors, personality traits, environmental elements and genetic components that cannot be isolated. No single factor causes OCD; rather, there exists an interaction between multiple causes that work together to create this disorder.

However, there is no definitive gene that causes OCD. Some individuals develop an inclination toward OCD which then becomes activated by certain life events.

It may have been inevitable for OCD to take hold, no matter the circumstances and events of life. While some people can remember beginning some symptoms of OCD during childhood, most experience them during their 20s.

Acknowledging the Cause Isn't Enough to Cure OCD

Sometimes, traumatic experiences and negative life events may contribute to the development of OCD in individuals. But simply exploring these events psychologically won't do any good - you still need to heal from those psychological explorations in order to truly find healing.

Psychological explorations are therapeutic approaches, such as psycho-dynamic psychotherapy. These seek to uncover your past life and subconscious in order to find a path towards emotional healing. The primary goals of these types of therapies are to gain insight into your hidden motivations so doctors or therapists can craft insightful directed therapies accordingly.

Previews alone aren't enough. Patients with OCD tend to be introspective and have already spent considerable amounts of time reflecting on the origin of their disorder. This ruminating could also be considered a type of mental compulsion, compounding any existing symptoms.

Many therapists make the mistake of encouraging their patients to reflect on triggering events, which only serves to further exacerbate their disorder. There is no guarantee that discovering the source of an issue will provide a solution for resolving it; finding the source may simply create more issues for you to manage.

Chapter 3: Why Has Nothing Worked?

OCD is an anxiety disorder that inhibits compulsive behaviors and intrusive thoughts. It may be mild in some individuals, or more serious for some. Patients suffering from OCD often become fixated on certain thoughts they don't even want to consider.

They may find it impossible to suppress these intrusive thoughts. Some OCD sufferers exhibit compulsive behaviors such as checking that everything is in order, counting whatever possible, or repeating tasks until their mind believes they have completed them "the right" number of times.

People may not enjoy this, but they cannot control their thoughts, emotions or actions. Untreated OCD can have a severe negative impact on your life; don't underestimate its power!

Different treatments exist for obsessive-compulsive disorder (OCD). Unfortunately, about 1/3 of people with OCD develop treatment-resistant symptoms.

This type of OCD doesn't respond to traditional treatments such as psychotherapy and medications. In this chapter, I will address treatment-resistant OCD, its causes, and how to manage them effectively.

Why Is Your Medication Not Working?

Various medicines have been approved by the FDA to treat OCD; however, for some individuals (approximately one-third of all OCD patients), these treatments do not seem to provide relief.

These reactions may occur for various reasons, such as taking drugs, drinking liquor, skipping doses, taking other medications at the same time, body chemistry or genetics. Sometimes you need to experiment with various medicines and doses before finding one that works for you.

How to Cope With It?

Augmentation treatment strategies may be worth attempting. This approach increases the chances of eliminating OCD symptoms through the use of multiple medications instead of just one drug.

Why Is Psychotherapy Not Working for You?

Psychological treatments are widely used to treat individuals suffering from OCD. While most patients find relief through psychotherapy, some do not respond. There may be several reasons why your attempts at treatment don't succeed such as: * Lack of family support systems

* Lack of social services.

* Your relationship with your therapist may be lacking.

* You aren't receiving the right therapy.

* You lack mental readiness to receive treatment.

Coping With OCD?

* Consider exploring each of these intensive treatment programs. There are numerous successful psychological and medical therapies for treating OCD.

* Unfortunately, not every therapy works for every patient. Some do not experience any improvement as a result of these therapies. As a result, intensive OCD treatment programs have evolved.

* Consider clinical trials. Many clinical trials offer free treatments to people with OCD who haven't found success with other treatments yet, and some of these advanced therapies may be worth trying if your symptoms persist despite treatment attempts. * You should consider trying clinical trials - some are even free! * Take advantage of free resources like clinical trials when possible

* You can have brain surgery and psychosurgery. However, very few individuals with OCD suffer from severe enough symptoms for brain surgery. In order to effectively treat OCD, surgical procedures often involve inactivating certain regions of the brain that are responsible for triggering its symptoms.

* Up to 70% of patients who undergo brain surgery report significant improvement after the operation. Deep brain stimulation, however, appears to be highly successful but remains in its experimental stage and should only be used as a last resort.

Strategies to Combat Treatment-Resistant OCD

Here are some key strategies you should know -

Combination Therapy and Pharmacological Treatment

Augmenting with an antipsychotic proved successful for a few individuals. Individuals who had taken maximum SSRI monotherapy for more than 12 weeks were most likely to benefit from the combination.

Recently, a meta-analysis was conducted on the increase of second-generation antipsychotic augmentation. Risperidone was reported to be significantly better than placebo at decreasing depression and anxiety symptoms. You can continue taking this selective serotonin reuptake inhibitor (SSRI) for 3-6 months to see how your dose works for you.

Be sure to increase the dose to a level that is acceptable to your body, or even switch to another front line agent from another class of medication and augmenting with an SSRI. According to a meta-analysis of OCD SSRIs, high doses were found more effective than low or average ones. The most important issue here is your tolerance; higher dosages of citalopram may increase arrhythmia risks; thus, an FDA security warning has been issued against it.

CBT

Patients often prefer CBT over medication therapy. Combining pharmacotherapy and CBT has been found to be highly effective for treating OCD symptoms. Close monitoring of patient-family dynamics must take place to detect whether there is covert or overt maintenance of the condition.

Family members should receive specific instructions on how to interact with the patient, what to say and not say, and how to act around them. A follow-up should also be conducted in order to confirm if all instructions have been adhered to.

Chapter 4: Types Of Ocd

From obsessing over keeping things tidy to checking the lock multiple times before leaving home, there are various forms of OCD.

In this chapter, I will describe the different forms of OCD and the behaviors individuals experience when suffering from them.

Scary Obsessions

Your obsessions can range from bad thoughts and the need to keep yourself clean to hurting others and keeping everything in its proper place. Whatever it may be, having an obsession can lead to all kinds of distress and disruption in your life.

Compulsions OCD

Excessive obsessions can lead to compulsive behavior as a way of coping, which only serves to make matters worse.

Compulsive behaviors may include excessive praying, avoiding things, washing hands repeatedly, behaving impolitely and showing unnecessary aggression; monitoring things repeatedly for accuracy or making sure everything is in order; etc.

Sometimes people engage in compulsive behaviors to escape the guilt they have felt due to their obsessive thoughts.

Here are some OCD subtypes commonly observed among individuals:

Contamination OCD

If you suffer from contamination OCD, you may become overly worried about spreading germs or getting contaminated from a disease. This can cause great distress and anxiety for those affected by it.

Due to fear of infection, you may feel hesitant entering public places and even hesitate to shake hands with others. Therefore, you may continue washing your hands multiple times out of fear for germs to avoid spreading infection. As a result, you may avoid public restrooms, gatherings, etc.

You may become aggressive if someone brings anything close to you that you consider "filthy." Some even fear getting contaminated with another person's bad luck, breath, and negative emotions.

Common obsessions associated with contamination OCD include:

* You fear developing cancer, STDs and getting sick in general.

* You worry about spreading contaminants and diseases to others.

* You experience intense fear of body fluids such as sperm, saliva, blood, etc.

* You worry about dirt, dust, radiation, toxins and germs inhaling into your lungs or on surfaces.

Some common contamination OCD compulsions include:

* You engage in ritualistic behaviors such as repetition, knocking, praying or other illogical practices.

* You continue researching diseases and germs with an agenda.

* You begin to scratch yourself out of fear that something may be contaminated on you.

* You start using harsh chemical cleansers on your face in an effort to cleanse it effectively.

* You keep changing clothes frequently

* You discard everything you believe to be "dirty."

* You separate the "dirty" items from the "clean" ones.

* You regularly clean, shower, and rinse.

Responsibility OCD

When you experience responsibility OCD, you often feel guilty and anxious about your own decisions. You don't prioritize anything other than what benefits yourself.

Do you find yourself constantly worrying about the consequences of your decisions, both good and bad? Fear of unintentionally hurting others is an all-consuming fear for many?

You could end up taking on all the blame and responsibility for events that weren't your fault. You might start to believe that you are responsible for everything that occurs around you, even if they weren't even your fault. You might start believing you are a terrible person if this occurs to you.

Misconceptions about responsibility OCD include that people with it often believe their problems are caused by low self-esteem or because they care deeply for others.

Some common obsessions associated with responsibility OCD include:

* You worry about not being able to stop something bad from occurring.

* You worry you might injure others.

* You fear endangering someone by accident.

Some responsibility OCD compulsions include: * You believe yourself to be kind of vicious.

* You fear spiritual harming others and pray that this does not occur.

Perfectionism OCD

If you suffer from perfectionism OCD, you are always anxious that something will go awry. Your mind is constantly trying to ensure everything is perfect. You worry constantly that something will go awry; therefore, you strive for perfection in everything.

You strive to keep everything under control. You worry about what could go awry if even one thing goes awry.

Your performance or other people's behavior must always conform to a certain standard or rule. Furthermore, you may feel an intense urge to finish something quickly after beginning it, leading to anxiety and high blood pressure levels.

If you are suffering from perfectionism OCD, you may experience the following symptoms:

* Rewriting personal letters, business letters, project reports, e-mails, classroom assignments and essays to ensure they are "perfect."

* You could end up redoing all your work and spending too much time on

unimportant details, resulting in missed deadlines.

* You could even keep rewriting sentences to make them sound "perfect."

* You may need to keep seeking confirmation from others that your work is satisfactory; otherwise, you could become anxious.

* It could take several hours just to finish what you started, though that time doesn't need to be strictly enforced - just make sure nothing remains incomplete.

* You keep reviewing and reconsidering your decisions because you feel overwhelmed with the pressure to make the perfect choice.

* You might even put off certain tasks out of fear of not having enough energy or taking too long to do them right, leading to frustration.

Harm OCD

Do you ever feel the urge to hurt other people when experiencing intense emotions? If so, then you could be suffering from harm OCD. In this type of disorder, patients have aggressive thoughts about harming or doing something violent with others.

What would a normal person do if they had the thought of hurting others through anger? He or she would likely ignore that thought after acknowledging its unjust nature and taking steps to prevent it.

People with OCD, however, experience a different kind of thinking. Patients become preoccupied with fear - what if they do something wrong or lose control - rather than simply worrying about what could happen if they try it anyway.

They may resort to rituals and compulsions in an effort to reduce their anxiety. But these actions are only temporary; fear and anxiety return after a certain period, creating an endless cycle.

They need constant assurance that these thoughts are unfounded and mean little.

If you suffer from harm OCD, here are some symptoms you might experience:

* You could get violent images or thoughts in your head and worry that these might come true, * You may worry about harming others without realizing it through negligence

* You become terrified with the thought of inadvertently or intentionally harming yourself or others out of impulsivity * You might even consider yourself to be truly evil, with only your external personality serving as camouflage for an inner evil side; thus, fearful thoughts keep haunting you whenever this dark side emerges. Worrying can cause intense anxiety when it does.

Your obsessive thoughts may be so frustrating and difficult to suppress that in an effort to reduce stress, you engage in rituals or compulsive behaviors like:

* You hide potentially hazardous objects such as razor blades, ropes, drugs and poisonous chemicals to avoid the urge to use them against yourself or others.

* You regularly review your actions to guarantee that no harm was done to either yourself or others.

* You avoid watching news programs and violent videos to protect yourself from becoming too angry. That may be because looking at them triggers your violent side.

* You spend a great deal of time online searching criminal matters and offenders to see if there's anything in common between you two.

* You keep praying and practicing spiritual rituals to maintain control.

* You ask people if OCD patients can harm others or not.

Sexual Orientation OCD

This type of OCD occurs when individuals experience intense fear of becoming attracted to the same gender. They become fixated on what might happen if they developed feelings for that gender; otherwise known as HOCD (Homosexual Obsessive-Compulsive Disorder).

Signs of anxiety might include:* Worrying that your sexual orientation might shift.

* Fear that people might judge you as LGBTQ (gay).

* Anxiety about having sexual fantasies.

* You keep trying to convince yourself that you are not involved in the LGBTQ (gay) community.

* You frequently check if or not you feel aroused when around other people.

*You worry about what will happen if you don't get aroused when desired.

* You strive to fit in with those around you.

* You worry about losing control or developing feelings towards someone of similar sexual preference as yourself.

Paedophilia OCD

People with paedophilia OCD often experience sexual or unwanted thoughts about children. There is a distinct difference between those with regular paedophilia and those suffering from Paedophilia OCD.

Paedophilia occurs when someone has inappropriate thoughts about children and does not realize it is wrong; thus they engage in inappropriate activities with children. On the other hand, someone suffering from paedophilia OCD is acutely aware of its inappropriate nature but chooses to remain silent about it.

Although they know these thoughts are inappropriate, they still feel depressed, ashamed and guilty for them. Though they have no intention of harming a child, their dirty thoughts cannot help but invade their mind.

Some common Paedophilia OCD obsessions include:

* You fear you have assaulted a young adult or child before.

* You experience sexual arousal when around children.

* You experience overwhelming sexual thoughts about young adults or children.

Your obsessive thoughts become so stressful that you begin engaging in compulsive behaviors to reduce anxiety. Common compulsive behaviors associated with paedophilia OCD include:

* You question the legality and morality of being attracted to someone under 18.

* You believe yourself a bad and horrible person for having improper thoughts about children.

* You avoid social gatherings where children could be present.

Relationship-Themed OCD

While having concerns about your relationship or partner is normal, if these worries become obsessions that last all day then you could have relationship OCD.

Relationship OCD occurs when you begin to doubt your partner's loyalty and feelings for you. These doubts are completely unreasonable and irrational and can have detrimental effects on daily life. Some common obsessions associated with relationship OCD include:

* You never stop worrying if the person you're with is the right one for you.

* You experience second thoughts about whether or not your love for them is genuine.

* You worry constantly that you're not good enough for a relationship with your partner.

Some common relationship OCD compulsions include: * Setting rules for them that they won't follow leads you to believe the relationship won't work out.

* You seek the perfect kind of romance but can never seem to find it. **

* When having sexual relations with your significant other, you become frustrated due to a desire for passion.

* You keep reflecting and questioning the skills and qualities of your partner.

* You engage in conversations with friends about how their relationship is progressing, to compare it with yours.

* You strive to find the ideal relationship online.

* You take note of every detail in your relationship and continue to question its integrity.

Scrupulosity OCD

People with scrupulosity OCD often experience unwanted and intrusive urges, images, thoughts about violating their moral, ethical or spiritual beliefs. As a result they become excessively guilty, nervous and upset.

To relieve themselves of these feelings, many sufferers turn to compulsive behaviours such as excessive prayer or prevention. Scrupulosity OCD can be divided into religious scrupulosity OCD and moral scrupulosity OCD; let me provide an example for each type.

* Moral Scrutiny OCD - Imagine someone is sitting and conversing with friends when a

joke is made that no one laughs! Anxiety sets in as they constantly assess whether they have offended someone, made an inappropriate joke, and now whether people hate him for it. This leads to constant analysis of potential offender and inappropriate jokes as well as whether people actually hate the person afterward.

* Religious Scrupulosity OCD (or Religious OCD) - Imagine attending a religious service where someone reads out loud some religious dialogues. Suddenly, something in his mind causes him to feel guilty and ashamed; he starts thinking about what would happen if he went to hell, was an evil person or not, had to admit their fault or not, etc., etc., etc., etc., etc.,

Hyperawareness OCD

Individuals with hyperaware OCD tend to pay excessive attention to external stimuli. To them, certain things seem closer, brighter, louder or more distracting compared to other people's surroundings.

They don't intend to pay attention to those things, yet they become so distracted by them that they cannot help but pay attention.

Some common triggers for individuals suffering from hyperawareness OCD include oscillating fans, broken TV pixels, fluorescent light, other people's keyboard typing, screeching brakes, conversations among friends or strangers while watching television or highway noise. Hyperawareness may further be divided into subcategories like Misophonia (where people become overly aware of external sounds) and phonophobia (fear of a particular sound).

Some individuals with hyperawareness become overly obsessed with their own thought processes. If they find that they think too much, they often question why, and then feel guilty for doing so.

If you suffer from this kind of OCD, your focus may shift towards:

* Swallowing according to a specific pattern, quality, frequency and quantity.

* Positioning feet's and arms' arms.

* Posture.

* An experience of stitches, labels, adjustments, texture and weight of fabric against your skin.

* Feeling of situational context, consistency and heart beat sound.

* Eye floaters.

* Sensation of sound intensity and frequency while blinking

Some common hyperawareness OCD behaviors include: * Neglecting to pay attention to every detail around you.

* Distracting yourself with music.

* You use full consciousness and meditation to control your thoughts.

* You become too busy, becoming a workaholic, so that you do not pay attention to other undesirable things.

* You attempt to eliminate these thoughts through force.

* You alter everything in your wardrobe to escape certain feelings or sensations.

* You undergo repeated examinations by doctors to rule out any body dysfunctions.

Emotional/Mental OCD

People with emotional OCD often experience feelings of unease or unrest. They may become anxious, worried, worried, depressed, etc.

Action OCD

Action OCD is a type of OCD in which individuals worry that if they focus too much on something, it might come true. These individuals experience unwanted thoughts and become obsessed with the possibility that these predictions could come true.

Hoarding OCD

Individuals suffering from hoarding OCD find it extremely difficult to part with their possessions, no matter their true value. This disorder affects them physically, emotionally, financially and socially; impacting all areas of life.

Hoarders often feel that having too many possessions sets them apart from everyone else. Common items to be hoarded include clothes, food, home supplies, photographs, cardboard boxes, plastic bags, documents, magazines and newspapers.

Fear OCD

Fear OCD is the fear of having aggressive thoughts, hurting others or losing control. People suffering from fear OCD often feel guilty, conscious, anxious and responsible about these thoughts they experience. They may believe they're losing control or doing something wrong which could have terrible repercussions; their neglect could harm someone. If you suffer from fear OCD you might experience some of these symptoms:

* You call your partner several times a day to check on them and ensure everything is okay.

* You check all devices multiple times just to make sure they're all turned off.

* Before leaving the house, always double-check that the door is securely locked.

* You engage in superstitious behaviors such as repeating words, tapping or counting.

* You wash your hands frequently to eliminate contamination from objects and ensure there are no germs present.

Health, OCD

If you suffer from health OCD, you may be afraid of illness, death, physical or mental suffering. You may feel like there's something wrong with you but no one can diagnose what's wrong and getting the appropriate treatment; furthermore, you worry about what will happen if these diagnoses and treatments fail. Some symptoms associated with fear-based OCD include:

* To imagine you may be suffering from an incurable disease which has yet to be discovered.

* Believing that doctors could make errors while reading test reports.

* Worrying if your illness will go undetected.

* You mistakenly believe a sensation to be indicative of an illness when in reality, it could simply be an illusion.

* Believe that your lack of investigation into symptoms indicates an underlying underlying problem with yourself

* Feeling uneasy in the presence of someone suffering from an illness.

Reflect on whether or not you have overlooked a key symptom associated with any illnesses you are dealing with.

If you suffer from one of the OCD types listed above, do not ignore it. Without treatment, symptoms could worsen over time and delaying treatment won't do any good. Take action today: there are various treatment approaches available now - from psychotherapy to brain surgery - that can help treat OCD.

Overall, 32-70% of OCD patients show signs of recovery, showing that recovery is possible. Different treatments exist for treating OCD; in this chapter I'll cover some of the available solutions.

According to research, 32-70% of OCD patients experience remission. This suggests that recovery is possible. Individuals suffering from OCD can be treated in various ways; in this chapter I'll review some of the available treatments for curing this disorder.

Psychological Therapy

Cognitive behavioral therapy (CBT) is one such example of psychological therapy for OCD that has been proven to effectively reduce both the intensity and frequency of symptoms. This form of therapy can be particularly effective for individuals suffering from severe cases.

Nearly two thirds of patients who undergo CBT report a significant reduction in both intensity and frequency of OCD symptoms. Unfortunately, CBT can be quite costly; thus many people opt to receive it in health care settings or hospitals to save costs.

If you are receiving Cognitive-Behavioural Therapy in such settings, then the option of "group CBT" exists. While this may seem intimidating at first glance, group CBT has its own advantages.

Sometimes, when you realize you are not alone and there are many others with symptoms similar to yours or even more severe than yours, healing can occur more quickly. An example is Exposure and Response Prevention (ERP). Other treatments include imaginary exposure, Habit Reversal Training, etc.

Cognitive-Behavioural Therapy (CBT)

CBT is a psychotherapeutic treatment designed to help individuals recognize and modify thought patterns that are disruptive, destructive, and negatively impact their lives.

CBT's primary goal is to alter your automatic negative thoughts, which may otherwise lead to anxiety, depression and other emotional difficulties.

Cognitive behavioral therapy (CBT) works to identify, challenge and transform negative thought patterns into rational and positive ones. There are various forms of CBT available; they include:

* Cognitive Therapy: This therapeutic approach aims to recognize and alter harmful thinking patterns, behaviors, and emotional reactions.

* Dialectical Behaviour Therapy: This therapeutic approach primarily addresses behavioral and psychological problems, while also emphasizing strategies such as mindfulness and emotional regulation.

* Multimodal therapy: This therapy suggests that psychological issues should be treated by addressing seven distinct but interrelated modalities. These include biologic/drug

considerations, interpersonal factors, cognition, imaging sensation behavior and effect.

* Rational Emotive Behaviour Therapy (REBT): This process helps identify all irrational beliefs, challenges those beliefs, and encourages you to confront and alter them.

Throughout CBT, people may face several difficulties. Some patients report finding it extremely difficult (if not impossible) to alter harmful or destructive thoughts after having identified them.

* This process is highly structured. It does not aim to address underlying unconscious resistances; rather, it provides patients with a focused and tailored treatment approach.

* Treatment alone will not provide results unless you're willing to make changes. In order for any treatment plan to work for you, there must be a strong dedication to making positive changes.

* Analysing one's emotions and thoughts requires a considerable amount of energy and time. Unfortunately, this self-analysis can be daunting for many individuals; however, in order to maximize its benefit we must commit the necessary effort and time.

Exposure and Response Prevention (ERP)

CBT encompasses many similar therapies. ERP is one such example. The process consists of two parts: exposure and response prevention.

This treatment primarily exposes you to various situations, objects, pictures and thoughts which are responsible for initiating your obsessions or creating anxiety.

The Response Prevention component of this treatment primarily aims to assist you in making a choice not to engage in compulsive behavior after your obsessions or anxieties have been activated--this process is typically administered by an experienced therapist at the start.

Eventually, you should be able to perform ERP exercises on your own. If you are an OCD patient, chances are you have already tried to confront your obsessive thoughts to see if it helps.

ERP ensures that when you address these thoughts, you also commit to yourself that you will do everything in your power to prevent yourself from succumbing to compulsive behaviors. By stopping these habits, you will notice a marked reduction in your anxiety levels.

Traditional psychotherapy or talk therapy helps the patient gain insight into their actual issues. Psychotherapy can be highly effective for treating certain conditions, however it is not typically successful when treating OCD.

OCD requires more than just awareness; ERP helps you recognize, address, and commit to change.

Imaginal Exposure

Some people are not yet ready to face reality. Imaginal exposure helps prepare them by creating an imaginary scenario that intentionally raises anxiety levels in the patient. This process helps prepare them for ERP.

For instance, if someone is obsessed with walking a certain way, the therapist may show them a picture of someone doing it differently. This will trigger their anxiety, and the therapist can assess its level.

Eventually, they will adapt to anxiety and become accustomed to it. This will reduce their fear over time, eliminating any strong repulsion towards it and making them more open to trying something new or difficult like ERP.

Habit Reversal Training

This training process incorporates relaxation techniques, positive reinforcement, social support networks, competition for response introduction and awareness training.

Awareness training involves recognizing the habits and sensations that take place in your body before engaging in specific compulsive behaviours. By recognizing these triggers, you will become more alert to any changes that take place prior to engaging in compulsive behaviors.

Habit Reversal Training

This training process incorporates relaxation techniques, positive reinforcement, social support networks, competition for response introduction and awareness training.

Awareness training entails recognizing the habits and sensations that take place in your body before engaging in specific compulsive behavior. Once identified, you can be more alert to any changes occurring within yourself mentally or physically before the onset of compulsive behaviors.

By working together with your therapist, you and they will find a way to manage or even stop your habits without anyone noticing. Here comes the competing response. In this section, the two of you will collaborate to come up with an alternative solution that won't cause too much noticeable disruption in your daily routine.

If you suffer from a vocal tick, exercising the muscles around your mouth and cheeks can help combat this habit. If symmetry touching things causes an urge, try doing it with another hand or tightly holding something against your body to break the compulsion.

Patience and commitment are necessary for this procedure to be successful; unfortunately, patients with severe OCD cannot benefit from it. Furthermore, since this process takes so long to complete, family support is necessary in order to successfully implement it.

ACT (Acceptance and Commitment Therapy)

This psychological therapy was recently discovered to be effective in treating OCD and certain anxiety disorders. The main premise behind this approach is that anxiety is an integral part of life, so how you respond to it matters greatly.

Other Treatments

Most OCD patients recover from front-line treatments. Unfortunately, some never fully recover from any of these treatments; this condition is known as "OCD-resistant treatment" and only a minority of individuals experience it.

Chapter 5: Self-Assessment

Self-assessment is of vital importance for people of all ages and in all professions. By being objective about ourselves and the actions we take, it becomes much simpler to identify areas for improvement or immediate attention.

We will be able to learn from all our past errors and recognize our progress over the years.

Though becoming objective towards one's own actions can be a challenging practice, if one gets into the habit of critically assessing one's decisions and actions, they will likely grow into much more confident individuals who take responsibility for their choices and commitments.

Self-assessment offers many advantages that should be recognized by everyone.

*Evaluating one's own actions gives us confidence, increasing security in our decisions. Through self-assessment, we eliminate any uncertainties that might be lurking beneath the surface as we reflect upon our work more critically; this in turn reduces any pressure from failure or uncertainty that might exist due to insecurity.

* Assessing one's own work helps a person finish it more quickly, since they will have a clearer idea of how things should be done. This makes for faster progress overall.

* Self-assessment helps people identify what they desire and are not interested in, enabling them to make better choices without making costly errors. By understanding one's strengths, they can use them effectively for personal gain.

* When someone assesses themselves, they become open to constructive criticism and changes. Evaluating our own actions will show us where we can make improvements in order to enhance our lives and progress further. It helps us break away from

outdated superstitions and become better individuals.

* Self-evaluation helps us become the best version of ourselves. By giving ourselves constructive criticism and striving for improvement, we can move past any limitations or shortcomings we might have and strive to reach new heights in every area. Ultimately, self-evaluation becomes the ultimate teacher; helping us improve ourselves further while becoming the most valuable version of ourselves possible.

* As we become a more self-assured version of ourselves, self-assessment provides us with opportunities to capitalize on our strengths and spend less time worrying about things for which we don't have clarity. It allows us to maximize efficiency in all areas of life instead of wasting energy on things that don't matter.

If someone is suffering from Obsessive Compulsive Disorder, self-evaluation can be a great tool to keep their OCD under control or even help them come out of it.

Most often, individuals are unaware that they possess OCD until it becomes an integrated part of their lives and they struggle to acknowledge when things become too much for them.

That is why, if they take a step back to evaluate their actions, it might become simpler for them to identify what went wrong and how to fix those issues.

Anyone suffering from OCD often obsesses over doing things a certain way and makes up stories to justify their preference. This can lead to miscommunication and conflict within the family, as well as physical problems when things don't go according to plan.

By critically assessing one's actions, they will become aware of these things and it becomes easier for them to try and change how they act.

That is why we have created this MCQ test for everyone - so they can assess their current situation and take control of their future. Anyone is welcome to take this assessment, and we hope providing honest answers to the questions given will be of immense assistance to anyone reading it.

Before we dive in, let us emphasize that there is no right or wrong answer; it all comes down to personal preference. So be honest with yourself and select the response which comes naturally to you.

* Do you find it difficult to stop thinking about something, or are you embarrassed of what you think and find it difficult to share these feelings with others?

(a)Yes (b)NO

* Do you experience any unpleasant thoughts which you are unable to stop?

(a)YES (b)NO

* Do you have an annoying habit, such as washing something over and over again or repeatedly checking locks?

Yes/No

* Do you tend to repeat yourself even if your answer was already correct on the first attempt?

(a)YES (b)NO

* Do you spend most of your time cleaning up after yourself and organizing/rearranging things in a special way?

(a)YES (b) NO

* Do you ever feel worried when things in your environment don't meet your expectations?

Chapter 6: Cognitive Behaviour Therapy Or Cbt For Ocd

OCD is a serious issue that should be treated with the utmost respect and consideration. There are various treatment options available to address the condition.

Here, I am going to focus on a specific treatment approach - "Cognitive Behavioural Therapy," or CBT."

What Is CBT?

Cognitive behavioural therapy (CBT) is a psychotherapeutic treatment. This allows people to recognize disruptive or destructive thought patterns (which can have detrimental effects on physical and mental health) and work toward changing them.

Negative thought patterns, if left unbroken, can have an adverse effect on your emotions and behaviors. Cognitive behaviour therapy specializes in changing these self-destructive thoughts which could otherwise contribute to furthering anxiety, depression, and emotional difficulties.

Cognitive-behavioral therapy seeks to identify, challenge and replace negative thoughts with more realistic and objective ones.

Cognitive Behavioural Therapy Types

Cognitive behavioral therapy (CBT) encompasses a wide variety of approaches and techniques for dealing with behaviors, emotions and thoughts. From structured psychotherapy to self-help materials - CBT has it all covered. CBT also offers various treatment approaches.

Cognitive therapy: Cognitive therapy is one of many cognitive behavioural therapies developed by Aaron T. Beck, CT and it belongs to this broader category.

Cognitive therapy is typically of a short duration. It operates on the idea that how you feel about certain things directly influences your emotional reactions.

Instead of dwelling on past experiences, this therapy focuses mainly on communication, behavior and present thinking. As a goal-oriented program, its primary objective is to help clients address issues.

Cognitive therapy has been demonstrated to be successful in treating personality issues, substance abuse issues, eating disorders, fear, panic, anxiety, depression and OCD (ocd).

Cognitive therapy, also referred to as "Behaviour therapy," has the primary goal of altering how you think and act - in other words, altering your behavior.

Dialectical Behaviour Therapy: Dr Marsha Linehan and her colleagues developed this process when they realized that cognitive behavioral therapy as a whole wasn't successful in treating some patients.

Due to this, they added some techniques and customized the process for patients' individual needs.

This type of evidence-based psychotherapy proved successful in treating borderline personality disorders by teaching people how to live in the present moment.

Counseling also assists in cultivating healthy ways to build and nurture relationships, manage emotions and manage stress.

If you struggle with self-destructive behaviors and emotional regulation issues, DBT could be the ideal treatment for you. It has even been known to be successful in treating PTSD (post-traumatic stress disorder).

Multimodal therapy: Arnold Lazarus developed this technique, which is a psychotherapy approach rooted in cognitive-behavioural therapy.

Human beings are biological creatures that interact, imagine, sense, act, feel and think; thus a comprehensive treatment approach must encompass all these modalities.

Assessment and treatment should address seven dimensions of personality: biology/drugs, interpersonal relationships, cognition, imaging, sensation, affect and behavior. Multimodality therapy relies on the idea that each modality must be addressed separately in order to treat different mental disorders. Every dimension of personality is affected differently depending on each individual; accordingly treatment must take into account this fact if it's going to be successful.

Rational Emotive Behaviour Therapy (REBT) was pioneered by Albert Ellis. This process helps you recognize negative thought patterns and irrational beliefs that may have an impact on your behavior and emotions.

Once you have identified these, a therapist can assist in developing strategies to replace those negative thought patterns with rational ones.

REBT can be beneficial in treating sleep issues, aggression, eating disorders, procrastination, overwhelming feelings (rage, guilt or anger), phobias, addictive behaviours, anxiety and depression - just to name a few!

Cognitive Behaviour Therapy's Impact

CBT emphasizes that feelings and thoughts play a major role in shaping behavior. For instance, someone who spends most of their time worrying about air disasters, runway accidents and aircraft crashes is likely to avoid flying altogether.

Cognitive Behavioural Therapy's primary purpose is to teach individuals that while they cannot control everything that happens around them, they do have control over their reactions and thoughts about those events. Over the last decade, Cognitive Behavioural Therapy has grown increasingly popular due to several reasons; including:

* CBT can help people recognize and change destructive thought patterns, leading to healthier ones.

* If you are searching for a quick-acting treatment option that's highly effective, cognitive behavioural therapy could be your ideal pick.

* If CBT proves successful for you, there will be no longer need for other psychoactive drugs.

** Studies have demonstrated its effectiveness in treating OCD and certain mental health disorders.

* Additionally, its cost effectiveness makes CBT an economical alternative compared to other costly treatments.

What Are The Advantages of Cognitive Behaviour Therapy?

Cognitive behavioral therapy offers many advantages. Some of them include:

* People suffering from OCD often hope their condition will improve and they won't have to spend their lives in misery. Unfortunately, people living with this disorder or other mental health issues often become pessimistic when thinking about their future prospects.

They find it difficult to imagine a time when their lives will not be disrupted by this disorder. CBT offers them hope and encourages them to strive towards positive changes in their future lives, helping them understand that while some actions may not be ideal, your reactions might not always be accurate and that you shouldn't give up on yourself; rather, try to address these behaviors so you can change them for the better.

* Cognitive behavioural therapy can also increase your self-confidence. Many people suffering from OCD or other mental health issues typically have very low self-esteem, which often contributes to why they struggle so quickly when trying to recover. Low self-worth feeds into all the negative thought patterns that shape one's behavior - but cognitive behavioral therapy has the potential to disrupt this particular model.

* As a result, you build confidence in yourself and begin to believe in your abilities. Once you gain clarity over how your thoughts operate and how they can be controlled, it becomes possible to alter your entire belief system.

Cognitive behavioural therapy (CBT) is known to give patients a feeling of relaxation. CBT helps you learn how to regulate your responses to symptoms by employing various relaxation techniques that develop quieter reactions; as a result, triggers are avoided more frequently, leading to reduced symptoms over time.

Cognitive behaviour therapy helps you develop rational thinking. The main benefit of this therapy is that you gain control over your thoughts. Sometimes cognitive distortions may happen unintentionally, but with practice you begin to question these disruptive thought patterns and become aware of their origin.

* By doing this, you become empowered to replace negative thoughts with positive and rational ones. Negative emotions no longer have control over you and allow rational assessment of a situation as well as an appropriate response.

* CBT provides mental support as you recover from this condition. Knowing that someone is available to talk about your problems at any time helps motivate patients to improve. When patients know there is someone there to assist them when

needed, they become motivated to improve.

* Individuals with OCD or other mental health problems often become triggered by anger. Anger then fuels compulsive behaviors, leading to frustration, shame and guilt over their thoughts. Cognitive Behavioural Therapy (CBT) seeks to address the underlying problems that cause these intense emotions by teaching you strategies for managing those responses while helping identify what's causing your anger and providing insight into its source.

* Cognitive behaviour therapy (CBT) can improve communication skills. OCD often comes along with social anxiety, addiction or depression and it can be hard to express yourself to other people when there are so many things going on that it becomes difficult to find the words to convey how you really feel. As a result, maintaining personal or professional relationships becomes much harder. CBT allows you to

speak from the heart without becoming angry, ashamed or guilty - providing an outlet for authentic expression of thoughts and feelings.

Cognitive behavioral therapy (CBT) has long been known to increase your adaptability. Many mental illnesses arise from an inability to cope with difficult circumstances like trauma, grief, confusion, aggression and frustration; CBT helps you develop the strength to manage these things so you stop bottling up emotions and start opening more doors for dealing with tough times. This ultimately aids you in handling stressful scenarios better.

* Cognitive Behaviour Therapy (CBT) also protects patients from relapse. Relapse often occurs among those suffering from mental health problems, and CBT provides a variety of tools to assist them in avoiding these incidents. CBT helps people recognize their underlying condition and how best to manage it; they thus understand destructive

thoughts they should strive to avoid; by doing this you automatically prevent yourself from relapsing.

Pitfalls to Avoid When Treating OCD Patients with CBT

Pitfalls When Treating OCD Patients With CBT

People facing Cognitive Behavioural Therapy face a variety of obstacles during the process.

Change Is Hard

Many patients report that simply acknowledging harmful and irrational thoughts does not provide them with any relief. Even when aware of how these patterns impact their daily lives, they remain unable to make changes. Replacing pessimistic thoughts with constructive ones may not always be possible even when one is aware of its detrimental effects on one's wellbeing.

Cognitive Behavioural Therapy Is Structured

CBT does not aim to alter underlying unconscious resistances like other treatment approaches do, rather it focuses on solving the root of all problems and requires guidance from an instructor. Although more in-depth, CBT tends to move slowly and be structured in its execution; unlike other therapeutic approaches which aim at relieving symptoms alone. The slower nature of CBT makes it a slower and more structured process overall.

How Is ERP Different From Traditional Psychotherapy (or Talk Therapy)?

Psychotherapy involves talking with patients to gain awareness and an understanding of their problem and its underlying cause. While psychotherapy can be highly successful in treating many mental illnesses, OCD requires special considerations.

Psychotherapy may be part of the treatment for OCD patients, but it should never replace ERP when it comes to treating this disorder.

Exposure Ritual Prevention and Awareness Exercises

It is essential to comprehend how exposure ritual prevention and awareness (ERPA) exercises affect symptoms. To better comprehend this relationship, let us look at a series of events that occur during an OCD spike - commonly referred to as an OCD spike.

First, there must be a trigger; something in your physical, social and mental world that triggers an obsession - painful thoughts or feelings that become overwhelming. At almost the same time you may experience fear, guilt, apprehension, fear, anger or any combination of these negative emotions.

These three events - exposure to a trigger, activation of an obsession and feelings of distress - are perceived as one cohesive unit. As such, terms like "trigger", "obsession" and "distress" are often used interchangeably when referring to this seemingly singular climax.

Your instinct may be to turn it off at once. Through trial and error, however, you may discover that by repeating some actions or mental gymnastics you can find temporary relief until another obsession strikes.

ERPA exercises address each event directly. First, you identify a trigger that causes obsession and compulsive behavior; then you practice exposure to this stimulus. The next step involves abstaining from rituals while cultivating awareness of distressing feelings.

Once this is accomplished, the distress will vanish. No longer do those obsessions cause such fear but instead become insignificant and repetitive; without obsessions there can be no need for compulsion.

To prepare for an exposure exercise, select a trigger: an obsession or compulsion that you wish to remove.

Practice exposure by creating an obsession with reality and imagination.

Practice ritual prevention by avoiding compulsion-inducing behaviour like fear-blocking.

Practice acceptance; fully inhabit the thoughts, pictures, impulses, emotions and physical sensations that arise as a result.

Selecting an Obsessive-Compulsive Combination for Elimination

When trying to eliminate obsession and compulsion from your life, choose one combination that is least distressing. Even if it takes some effort, begin with something that offers the greatest chance of success.

Exposure, Tapping Into Obsessions

Exposure involves coming into contact with triggers of obsession in reality that exist outside our physical and social world, or imagined situations that take place inside our mind. Fear can be both the problem and solution to dealing with fear; although dealing with fear can be frightening, it's necessary for success.

On a case-by-case basis, patients reported that once they started managing their anxiety, it wasn't as painful as expected. Most importantly, however, is that exposure seems to work; obsessions no longer trigger fear but become mere "thoughts". Since these thoughts have no emotional charge, they become unimportant and eventually fade away completely.

Remember, exposure exercises should be performed gradually as you work toward your desired result. This type of gradual progress is known as shaping.

Begin with something that causes minimal stress and stay there until there is little or no response. Only then, move onto another situation that is only slightly more challenging than the first, and stay until all distress has disappeared.

This process will continue until all your obsessions, even those you found most frightening at first, have been fully explored.

Once you reach your destination, you will have become desensitized from previous exposure exercises and so the final stage won't be as difficult as the beginning. This practice of taking small steps towards achieving a goal is an essential component of recovery.

Two conditions must be fulfilled for fear to be eradicated: we must avoid rituals and other measures that cause us harm; additionally, the use of false fear blockers is discussed further in the following section.

The second requirement is the need for prolonged exposure. Your exposure sessions must be long enough that you experience a marked reduction in distress during exposure.

Your sessions may last an hour or longer. What most people experience during these times is a gradual increase in stress that becomes stable after some minutes and then starts to decrease. During this phase, you will begin to reap the rewards of exercise.

Whatever the trigger, exposure alone will quickly diminish its power to cause fear. Over time, you will notice that fear levels begin to decrease until there is little or no discomfort left. By eliminating this trigger from your life, you have neutralized its effect and learned that exposure alone can provide lasting relief from anxiety without needing harmful fear blockers.

Limit your exposure sessions to no more than 90 minutes by selecting triggers of easy to moderate difficulty.

Exposure can be draining mentally and emotionally, so you don't want to create unnecessary issues by overextending yourself. If you underestimate the strength of a trigger and find that it takes longer than 90 minutes for stress levels to decrease, stop working on it and replace with another simpler exercise.

Once desensitized from these exercises, you can revisit those situations you previously underestimated. As previously noted, exposure exercises can either be real or imagined. Reality exposure aims at eliminating obsessions caused by real situations in both physical and social environments; such activities require being physically present in those trigger situations.

Exposures in the imagination are meant to dispel obsessions caused by thoughts and images of future events that seem impossible or unlikely. To achieve these effects, which exist only within your head, you must come into contact with imaginary triggers.

One of the best ways to stimulate your imagination is writing down the contents of your obsessions and audiotaping that situation for as long as necessary until you feel some relief. Alternatively, rewrite and read it over an extended period until stress begins to dissipate.

When engaging in any exposure exercise, it is imperative not to stop when your anxiety grows. Doing so will prevent desensitization and may even make you more aware of the situation you are trying to escape from.

Plan your exposure sessions for times when you will have plenty of time to finish and won't be interrupted or distracted. To achieve better results, practice every day - including weekends and holidays! Doing this makes practicing easier with faster outcomes. Additionally, start doing the exercises early in the day to reduce any potential distractions or delays.

Ritual Prevention Refraining from False Fear-Blocking Behaviour

A fake fear blocker is any act or thought that immediately follows an obsession that decreases fear. I use the term "false" because any decrease in fear is temporary and usually returns after some period of recovery. The primary disadvantage to this strategy is that it prevents exposure, thus hindering recovery.

Mental rituals, or intentional words and images you tell yourself, can also be overcome. The question should not be "Can I prevent rituals?" but rather: Am I willing to prevent them?" If your goal is to overcome OCD, the answer should be yes; even if there is some initial fear involved in discontinuing these practices, the long-term benefits of not having OCD outweigh any short-term inconvenience.

The age-old saying, "It's easier than you think," has been proven true by those who have broken free of ritualistic stress and found success. You too can join their ranks by designing your exposures accordingly; controlling your anxiety levels allows for easier performing rituals without distraction becoming one of your first false fears.

Focusing on something else, they hope to distract themselves from the obsessions related to anxiety and distress. Being fully conscious of one's actions, being actively engaged, and moving can all be ways for those with an energetic tendency to compete with repetitive intrusive thoughts and images. Listening to music or speaking without thought are methods used by some who attempt to lessen the effects of obsessions.

Worriers often turn their focus towards mundane daily issues in an attempt to escape their worries. But the most extreme and hazardous distraction may be self-inflicted injuries, often to the head, as if casting out demons, making amends for guilt, or exchanging physical suffering for emotional anguish.

Distractions offer only temporary relief from uncontrollable, often unpredictable obsessions. Exposure is the real fear blocker and avoidance only hinders recovery; exposure is essential for true transformation.

Before you knew this, however, you likely did what came naturally and avoided triggers that activated irrational images or thoughts. Now is the time to take control of your recovery path; fear can be an ally when recognized as triggers for obsessions and desensitization targets. Once these have been neutralized so you can approach them comfortably again, success has been proven!

Reasoning is the most commonly employed fear blocker, though most of the time the individual understands that their fears are unreasonable. Unfortunately, during acute OCD flare-ups this understanding may wane and doubts may arise that our thoughts could actually be true - such as "I have a major character flaw or I am mad!" Just as nature abhors emptiness, humans also dislike uncertainty.

We attempt to manage OCD through rationalizing, analysing, intellectualizing and theorizing in an attempt to gain clarity. Unfortunately, OCD often results when fear blockers cause us to imagine things incorrectly or question unreasonable thoughts without foundation. Unfortunately, these efforts often prove ineffective.

We often lack direct control over how we react emotionally. Although rational fear has a low threshold for rational control, OCD sufferers often succumb to compulsive behaviors that divert our focus away from rational thought processes. Studies have even found that connections between brain emotional systems and rational systems are stronger than those between them (LeDoux, 1996).

Scholars, poets and other great individuals have shared this understanding throughout history; today neuroscientists are adding their insights about how the mind functions. Remember: what you think doesn't help you; doing is what will.

Assurance is one of the most powerful and unrecognized fear and recovery blockers. I've noticed it in over 90% of people, who often seek reassurance to soothe their OCD or anxiety. Since so many suffer from obsessive-compulsive disorders, this deserves special consideration as people with these disorders fear that their obsessions may materialize.

To reduce their distress, they often enlist the help of family or close friends to assure them that their fears will not come true. As obsessions tend to be unrealistic, family members or close friends (and even therapists) can offer assurances that there is nothing to fear and nothing wrong will occur.

People who fear being irresponsible or reckless often request insurance that is unnecessary. While this may provide them with some temporary comfort, the fear of not being accepted leads them down a path toward recovery - this is known as the first paradox.

Reassurance is never ideal - it can actually do more harm than good. But for some people, temporary relief from anxiety or stress is so satisfying that they find themselves continually searching for more, creating an impossible paradox: The more reassurance one receives, the greater their desire for more of it. Meeting this demand is no different than trying to fill a bottomless well.

Constant demands for comfort can not only hinder recovery, but also become imposing demands that lead to interpersonal conflicts. In one case, a woman's husband's inquiries became so intense and frequent that she moved out and rented an apartment on her own.

Paradox number three. Once the need for reassurance is removed, there is no longer any desire to seek it out, along with a reduction of obsessions and other compulsives.

So how do you deal with your desire for reassurance?

First and foremost, stop asking for it. Identify and avoid asking your most frequent questions, as these could indicate obsessions that were taking control of you - they become non-verbal requests that he would give immediately when needed. That way, you won't feel so guilty when others notice them either! For instance, one client I worked with would suddenly stop doing whatever she was doing, sit down, and space out - these behaviors became clear indicators that she needed help managing her obsessions instead of asking her husband directly for assurance which he could give immediately upon detection.

His cue to tell her not to worry was his way of telling her her fears were unfounded and it was all due to her obsessive-compulsive disorder. In addition to direct requests, subtler ones must also be addressed and put an end to.

Second, make your friends and family aware of the detrimental effects of comforting others. Make sure they read this passage, emphasizing that comfort is not a substitute for recovery.

Third, craft a polite refusal statement. Even if you try to avoid it, those who usually reassure you may still attempt to give assurance. Therefore, work together with those who usually give assurance to create an acceptable way of saying no; one strategy is saying, "I believe I want to be reassured. Reassurance should never be relied upon; instead, seek ways to keep reassurance at bay." Reassurance does not always lead to peace of mind but can often lead to further anxiety.

"That's why I won't answer.' If this approach fails, it could be that the agreed upon statement itself has become comforting or that you think nothing wrong will occur because your assurances would alert you. In such cases, the best course of action would be to stop talking entirely about OCD altogether.

Awareness

We've all heard that facing our fears is key to overcoming them. But this advice can be hard to follow through with; our instinctual reaction when faced with danger is usually fight or flight; however, in OCD you need to recognize and fight through all the feelings associated with OCD in order to survive. Part of overcoming OCD requires acknowledging and facing your fear head-on--feeling it, holding on, becoming involved--and eventually conquering it.

Reading it may cause anticipation to flare up, but remember that you can manage your anxiety by gradually approaching triggers so that only mild to moderate anxiety occurs. On contact, you may experience increased levels of fear at first, then stabilize and then decrease over time as the situation warrants.

At this stage, you can reap the rewards of your treatment. By becoming desensitized to fear, focus on feeling uncomfortable thoughts, emotions and physical sensations;

pay attention to scary images in your mind; accept these fears as much as possible while thinking positively about dreaded future events.

Say to yourself, "So be it." Imagine living in a world of uncertainty, never knowing if or when something bad will happen, never being free from worry, and so on. Keep thinking about these thoughts and casting images to intentionally create fear; this is how we use fear to combat it.

No amount of avoidance will ever bring you freedom from fear; only through facing it head on and becoming aware of your emotions and physical responses to it. Where do you sense fear in yourself? If your heart starts racing faster, pay attention.

Muscle pressure can be felt in many ways. Focus on breathing faster and louder; does your stomach/chest feel tight? Are you feeling hot/sweating? If the answer is yes, that means you are on the right path as fear has worn out and worn away; pursue fear and conquer it for good. All these unpleasant sensations serve a purpose!

After some exposures, you will know for certain that the fear is gone forever. Even when trying to invoke it, nothing works. Yet you may be worried that obsessions will grow stronger if you give up trying to stop blocking them or do them intentionally; or maybe you fear what could happen instead - however this does not always take place.

Instead, the opposite occurs; you will recover by training your brain's fear system to stop making false alarms about harmless events.

By desensitizing yourself to past anxiety triggers, you will begin to recognize them for what they truly are - harmless thoughts and images that are part of your normal stream of consciousness. In other words, OCD is erased when unwanted images and thought impulses are confronted and accepted.

Many may be asking: if exposure to anxiety is all that's necessary for OCD recovery, why hasn't this already taken place? After years of struggling with my obsessions, the answer lies in discovering why you keep coming back: you have used pointless fear blockers as a way of taking the stress away from these stressful thoughts.

Your fear exposures have not lasted long enough for them to naturally fade away due to how you're feeling. Once you finish completing your first exposure exercise, however, you will gain full insight into this subject.

Exercises like these can seem intimidating at first, but be aware of the rewards they bring: 1. Emotional changes due to less fear or no fear;2. Rational thoughts replacing irrational ones;3. Ability to maintain employment or volunteer activities;4.

Involvement in common interests and routines.

5. Enjoying fulfilling family and social activities and relationships

Cognitive Therapy

As previously discussed, cognitive therapy works to identify and alter thought patterns that cause negative behaviour, stress, or anxiety. Cognitive therapy helps you recognize when your brain is sending you false messages so you can interpret them differently and act differently so as to manage these obsessions more effectively.

Cognitive therapy consists of some outpatient sessions and homework for patients to do between sessions. If you suffer from severe obsessive-compulsive disorder, frequent therapy sessions with your therapist may be necessary.

Chapter 7: Exponential Therapy With Visualisations

There are various therapies, particularly behavioral ones, which can be effective for treating obsessive-compulsive disorder. While each therapy differs slightly from another in terms of technique or procedure, they all share one thing in common: effectiveness.

Typically, the primary aim of behavioral therapies like imaginal exposure therapy is to expose people with OCD to what they fear most: disturbing thoughts. Although these treatments have proven quite successful, only two-thirds of people suffering from mental conditions like OCD complete treatment.

Many patients fear exposure exercises because they perceive severe distress associated with them. Furthermore, many do not fully comprehend the logic or principle behind therapy-based treatments.

Unfortunately, individuals may experience difficulty adhering to the progress of treatments when things get tough. To improve success rates, it's beneficial to comprehend all elements of imaginary exposure therapy in advance.

Exposure therapy has been developed to assist individuals in confronting their personal fears. When someone feels threatened, they may attempt to avoid activities, situations or things that trigger fear in order to reduce uncomfortable feelings for a while; however, doing so could potentially make matters worse in the long run.

Psychologists can be invaluable in this situation. They will suggest the correct version of exposure and treatment to break through fear and avoidance patterns. Through exposure therapies, healthcare professionals help create a secure environment so patients can safely expose themselves to what they tend to avoid.

Individuals exposed to their feared activities or objects in a safe environment often report less fear and avoidance of those things. No matter what form of OCD you suffer from, imaginary exposure therapy is an invaluable skill that should be added to your arsenal. Here you will gain comprehensive knowledge on this effective treatment for Obsessive-Compulsive Disorder.

What Is Imaginal Exposure Therapy?

First and foremost, you should know that Imaginary Exposure Therapy has been scientifically proven to be one of the most successful treatments for OCD. But in order to fully comprehend this technique, one must have some basic understanding of Exposure Response Prevention (ERP).

Exposure and response prevention (ERP) is a type of cognitive behavioural therapy (CBT). Studies have consistently proven that it to be the most successful therapy for obsessive-compulsive disorder. ERP's primary principle involves repeatedly exposing an individual to their fears without performing any action related to compulsive anxiety reduction, in hopes that this will make them less afraid when faced with stressful situations.

Habituation is a psychological technique used to demonstrate that people with mental illness or other anxiety disorders become less fearful of certain situations if they keep facing them repeatedly.

If someone is afraid of touching doorknobs because they believe that doing so might spread any type of infectious disease, ERP can interfere by making them touch them repeatedly and not letting them rinse their hands afterwards. For example, if you worry about your house catching fire and check stove knobs frequently, ERP would let you use the stove but prevent checking once finished using it. The primary goal of ERP has been to alter different types of fear reactions through direct confrontation with affected individuals' behaviors.

Many individuals with OCD experience more distressing mental images and thoughts, rather than externally noticeable compulsive behavior. This is especially true for people suffering from Pure O or Pure Obsessional OCD; forms such as Harm OCD, Scrupulosity OCD, and Relationship OCD fall under this category.

For individuals suffering from any of the types of OCD, imaginary exposure therapy can be the most beneficial treatment. In this type of therapy, healthcare professionals will assist you in using your imagination to directly confront any fears or feelings associated with fear.

Imaginal Exposure Therapy, a straightforward treatment for obsessive-compulsive disorder, involves writing down or reading short stories related to the person's thoughts. However, these stories differ from other stories people enjoy reading.

These stories often revolve around the most horrific thoughts of those with OCD, leading to an unfavorable conclusion. Yet many people with OCD don't enjoy sharing stories about their worst case scenario - you might be surprised how few people actually enjoy writing them!

One common phenomenon with imaginary exposure therapy for treating obsessive-compulsive disorder is that many patients begin to cry or stop therapy when faced with reading and writing stories about their fears. Thus, only use imaginary exposure stories when someone feels ready to confront their most fearful thoughts. Another important element of this treatment plan is for both client or patient to feel secure during exposure procedures as well as feeling secure going places they believe are dangerous.

The purpose of imaginary exposure therapy is to make someone experience fear without running away, without comforting, neutralizing, destroying or distracting them from the situation. In such exposures, individuals are instructed to deal with their situation or fear mentally by visualizing or imagining it in their mind. For instance, if someone suffers from agoraphobia (fear of crowds), they might visualize standing or visiting a busy and congested shopping mall.

Though there are numerous reasons for engaging in imaginal exposure therapy, the primary one is that it provides an efficient means of exposure to obsessional thoughts that may not possess any visible compulsion. Furthermore, there are other reasons why this particular approach to exposure could prove successful; just take a look at some of them!

Certain actions and thoughts cannot be performed for ethical or legal reasons, such as nominating someone to commit murder or molestation against a small child.

Conjuring up a standard response to certain thoughts is not always straightforward. For those suffering from existential obsessive-compulsive disorder, for example, replicating nonexistence through behavioral exposures would likely prove impossible or absurd.

Some individuals can become very anxious when faced with certain thoughts. Many individuals with OCD are so deeply affected by stress or anxiety about a certain thing, circumstance, or incident that writing down short stories based on those fears may be an effective transitional step to help them face their fear more honestly.

No matter the motivation, imaginal exposure therapy can be highly effective for individuals suffering from OCD--if they prepare both for writing and using these imaginal exposures.

Facts About Writing Stories of Imaginal Exposure

First and foremost, these stories are written with the person's active involvement with OCD, and are entirely based on their true obsessions. For these tales to be highly effective, they need six specific characteristics. These attributes guarantee maximum impact - so take a look at these specific traits!

* When crafting stories, it is best to write in the present tense. Don't write as though an event occurred one year prior; write as though everything is happening right now. Similarly, describe any eventualities as though they will take place immediately afterwards.

* When crafting these stories, the first person must be used. Instead of writing "She pushed her boyfriend into the lake," you should write something like 'It was I who pushed my boyfriend into the lake."

Remember: your imaginative works have nothing to do with other people; it's solely personal.

* Stories must be grounded in reality. Only imagine to the degree that is convincing or trustworthy for you at first glance.

* An important characteristic of imaginary stories used for exposure therapy is that the author or patient should keep the stories true to life. That means if something in your current thoughts causes you distress or irritation, then write a story about it. Conversely, if the thought itself doesn't bother you at all then there's no need to waste precious time crafting an elaborate tale about it.

* Stories of imaginary exposure should be made as horrifically bad as possible, like the participant's worst nightmare. These could include eternal damnation for murdering your own child, or living the rest of your days with guilt that you sexually harassed

them. * Stories should also be told with extreme prejudice so as to create a realistic experience for all involved.

* An essential feature of an imaginary exposure story is its briefness. Keep in mind that this phase of therapy differs from any creative writing class; if you are obsessed with hurting someone, then your story needs to explore both this thought process as well as its potentially hazardous outcomes, where you must accept responsibility.

Writing stories for therapy should be relatively short compared to other creative or imaginative works; no more than 1/2 to 3/4 pages should you include. Your focus should be on sticking with the main content without resorting to metaphor or attractive adjectives; in other words, make your story powerful, even if it's only one sentence long or half a page in length.

Once someone with OCD has finished writing their story, they should read it aloud repeatedly and loudly. Many exposure therapists recommend that patients read their stories at least 30 times daily; however, you may be wondering how this is possible in light of everyone's busy lifestyle.

Don't fret, you can achieve your goal with these simple steps: read your story ten times before beginning work, another ten times during lunch break and the remaining ten times when done with work. No matter how hectic your schedule may be, remember to read at a steady pace and avoid fast reading.

The primary objective is for readers to experience the full impact of a story, so therapists advise against reading it quickly. In order to fully benefit from imaginary exposure therapy, it is necessary to go through exposure stories multiple times in order to see tangible and desired outcomes.

There is another effective alternative to reading your story every day. If you find that due to an overwhelming work or family commitments, you are unable to read as often as desired, then recording the short narrative allows for multiple listens so that all who hear it can enjoy it attentively.

Recording your story can be a great solution because you can listen to the recorded audio both on the way to work and when you get home. This way, you can organize your time more effectively. Sometimes reading or listening to a story until it becomes less intimidating or unbearably boring may actually be beneficial in some cases - that's when boredom kicks in!

Chapter 8: Take Action And Stay Mindful

Everyone is unique and faces different levels of difficulty, making it impossible for counsellors and psychologists to create a one-size-fits all solution. However, some less conventional solutions can be successful as some individuals with OCD respond quickly and correctly when exposed to these methods.

Obsessive-Compulsive Disorder, also known as OCD, is characterized by repetitive behaviors or compulsions based on an individual's obsessions. Obsessions refer to unwanted and intrusive thoughts that the patient attempts to suppress or deny repeatedly. These symptoms may get worse over time when trying to escape them by engaging in self-soothing techniques like denial.

Today, we will look at two methods of helping patients manage these intrusive thoughts: mindfulness and ACT (Acceptance and Commitment Therapy). Both techniques provide them with a new way of seeing things and confronting these thoughts head-on.

Mindfulness

Anyone suffering from OCD who seeks therapy or treatment must have come across the concept of mindfulness at least once during their journey. Mindfulness is simply trying to stay present in the moment without getting consumed by other thoughts that may come later on. Unfortunately, for people living with OCD, this may not be so straightforward.

People suffering from obsessive-compulsive disorder experience repetitive and intrusive thoughts throughout the day that cause them anxiety or obsession. To cope, some techniques have been taught to distract themselves from these thoughts or to calm fears caused by sudden bursts of insight.

Mindfulness, however, differs from these techniques in that it encourages patients to acknowledge their thoughts rather than trying to escape, suppress, or hide them.

Even those without OCD sometimes experience random thoughts that are unrealistic and cause them to feel threatened, just like those with OCD do. Yet how are the two groups different? Those without OCD simply accept these as other thoughts while obsessive-compulsive patients struggle to accept that these are simply thoughts in their head.

In essence, those suffering from obsessive-compulsive disorder become trapped in their inner thoughts and do not accept reality as it is. They interpret these feelings as warnings or danger signals; some even take these thoughts so far that they begin to view them as potential threats to themselves.

The difficulty arises in not being able to distinguish inner experiences from reality. Mindfulness, which urges us to stay present in the moment, provides tools and techniques for accepting these thoughts for what they are: mere ideas created by their creative mind. This technique requires patients to internalize the therapeutic concept that "it's just a thought".

Mindfulness therapy, also known as ERP (Exposure with Response Prevention), shares many similarities with ERP in that it asks individuals to acknowledge their thoughts and be aware of what triggers them. Once recognized, they are then instructed on how to not respond to those triggers in the future.

Mindfulness differs in that it requires patients to accept inner experiences without judgment or criticism. Furthermore, they must stay present and feel all thoughts, even if they may be painful or frightening, without doing anything about them; simply accept them as unreal thoughts that cannot be changed - thus making mindfulness therapy both challenging and effective for people suffering from ASD.

Mindfulness is often seen as an obstruction to other treatments for Obsessive-Compulsive Disorder, since it encourages acceptance of thoughts instead of pushing them away. Yet mindfulness can be combined with other treatments like CBT or ERP in order to maximize their efficacy. Furthermore, mindfulness may be combined with ACT (discussed in the next section) for even greater results.

This method of therapy relies on simply allowing thoughts to exist in the mind, no matter how painful they may be. These should not be attached to any judgement or weight and allowed to fade naturally or disappear. This can be implemented gradually (starting at a low level) and then gradually building it up over time. The first step in practicing this skill is keeping an open mind. Other ways to achieve it include exercising regularly, eating nutritiously, finding balance in work-life, and getting plenty of sleep each night.

* Maintaining a safe distance from toxic people and the environment.

* Paying attention to the language someone uses in daily life.

* Limiting alcohol consumption or discontinuing narcotic use.

* Ceasing the habit of trying to control intrusive thoughts, and maintaining balance in life.

Obsessive-compulsion disorder (OCD) is a disorder that can manifest in various ways and be triggered by many things, one of which being stress. The most effective way to improve your OCD skills is through learning and practicing relaxation techniques on a regular basis. Here are three easy techniques you can try on your own:

Deep Breathing

Deep diaphragmatic breathing or "abdominal breathing" sends an intense relaxation signal to the brain, effectively decreasing physiological excitement and thus stress levels.

To begin abdominal breathing, sit or lie down in a quiet environment with one hand on your chest and the other on your stomach. Some prefer to close their eyes for extra privacy, but this is not necessary. Breathe in slowly through your nose.

When you breathe in, feel your abdomen expand. You will know when this has occurred when the hand on your chest remains almost stationary while the one on your abdomen moves outward.

Once you've taken a deep breath, slowly blow air through pursed lips - like inflating a balloon - until your stomach drops back towards your spine. Only the hand over your stomach should move when this occurs.

Exhalation should last at least 2-3 times as long as inhalation. Deep breathing begins to provide relaxation after a minute or two, but for maximum benefits it should be done for five, ten, or even twenty minutes.

Mindfulness Meditation

Once you've mastered the deep breathing technique, try mindfulness meditation. This involves simply observing without judgement or rejection of thoughts.

By practicing mindfulness meditation, we become more aware of our thoughts and can better detach ourselves from them. Through this technique, we become less likely to be affected by disturbing thoughts like obsessions - which often accompany OCD. Indeed, mindfulness plays a crucial role in dealing with acceptance and commitment.

Start with the deep breathing exercise described above to practice mindfulness meditation. As you breathe in and out, pay attention to any thoughts, feelings, fears, anxiety or worries that pass through your head.

Simply be aware of your thoughts without trying to escape or suppress them. Pay attention to what happens if you leave them alone and let them go. Use deep breathing as a guiding principle throughout this exercise.

At first, mindfulness meditation may cause some degree of anxiety as you come face-to-face with troubling thoughts, fears and worries. But with practice comes comfort in just sitting there with these feelings without taking any action - making the practice an invaluable learning tool.

Progressive Muscle Relaxation

Progressive muscle relaxation (PRM) can also be combined with deep breathing for even greater muscle release. PRM helps identify hidden tension throughout your body and can provide lasting relief.

When practicing PRM, find a quiet room and begin the breathing exercise above. As with your inhalation, tighten all the muscles in your face. Hold for 10-20 seconds before slowly exhaling by breathing out slowly.

Repeat this multiple times and gradually work your way throughout your body - shoulders, arms, stomach, buttocks, legs and calves - by inhaling/pressing and exhaling/relaxing in this pattern.

Let us now examine how mindfulness enhances CBT's approach to treating OCD. Traditional CBT seeks to enhance three primary elements, or A's: acceptance, assessment and action. Mindfulness plays an integral role in this process by offering insight into:

Acceptance - OCD often causes individuals with the disorder to live in fear of their inner thoughts, which have created an entirely separate world within them. Pushing these thoughts away only serves to compound the anxiety and paralyze one's mind. Acceptance can make all the difference when trying to cope with daily life's pressures.

Accepting and acknowledging intrusive thoughts, physical sensations, or any other unpleasant emotion is the initial step in improving one's condition. To do this effectively, one must learn how to not attach meaning to these frequent thoughts or feelings and stop trying to alter or chase them away.

These objectives can be attained through mindfulness. How? By paying attention to the events around you in daily life; from listening for running water while taking a shower, to feeling the physical sensations experienced while sitting in a chair. Small details matter too - for example, taking notice of sounds around you while watching television or other distractions.

Other methods used in mindfulness include formal meditation, which helps the patient focus on anchoring. When dealing with OCD, this concept works by focusing on details like one's own heartbeat or breathing rate; doing this allows cogitation to occur naturally without judgement or explanation required. These strategies contribute to acceptance of CBT treatments overall.

Assessment - Traditional cognitive-based therapies focus on uncovering the distorted way of thinking that causes OCD. Mindfulness allows the individual to consciously cross that thought off their list and accept it with consent. For instance, someone suffering from OCD may have thoughts such as, "I am going to get sick because even after washing my hands once, they are still not free from germs".

Mindfully allowing a thought would mean to live within it, yet do so with an objective attitude, such as "My hands may not be completely clean from germs, so I cannot predict my future at this time."

Simply by changing one's perspective, they can stop performing compulsions (in our example, repeatedly washing hands to rid themselves of germs).

Before one can consciously accept certain thoughts, one must assess their seriousness. People with OCD often judge a situation without truly considering its significance and become trapped in fear of something uncertain. Therefore, rather than being afraid, we must first pacify our thoughts by placing them into an objective perspective.

Action - Once we have accepted and evaluated our thoughts of the inner world, the next step is to take necessary and effective measures against OCD. In traditional CBT, taking action often entails confronting fearful thoughts or performing certain compulsions.

Mindfulness can be a helpful tool in this step, as it enables one to accept unpleasant thoughts and images in their imaginary inner world. By accepting such scenarios, it becomes much easier for them to suppress compulsive behaviors.

Why choose mindfulness when treating OCD?

Studies on mindfulness for OCD have demonstrated its effectiveness. Integrating mindfulness into treatments has also been proven to yield better results. Examples of research supporting its use in treating OCD include:

*In 2010, three individuals with OCD were investigated to assess the efficacy of mindfulness therapy in treating their disorder. All three began by employing suppression mechanisms as a way of managing their symptoms.

The suppression mechanism suggested that rather than accepting thoughts, participants used coping mechanisms to push away unpleasant ones. After six sessions of mindfulness therapy, each participant was evaluated using the Yale-Brown Obsessive Compulsive Scale.

This assessment tool is designed to detect and quantify OCD symptoms. A study conducted through Y-BOCS demonstrated that after participating in mindfulness-based therapy sessions, they were much healthier than when they first began.

* In 2013, a larger study conducted among thirty patients confirmed the effectiveness of this therapy. All subjects were assigned to an heterogeneous group for testing purposes.

One group used mindfulness-based skills, while the other relied on coping mechanisms. After some time had passed, research revealed that those using mindfulness-based skills exhibited fewer compulsions than their counterparts whose urges to perform such acts remain mostly unchanged.

ACT, Acceptance and Commitment Therapy

Acceptance and Commitment Therapy (ACT) is a third-wave behavioural therapy that has been around for some time but recently gained mainstream media attention. This type of mindfulness treatment offers relief from many problems including OCD. Compared to traditional CBT, ACT helps patients identify and accept challenging thoughts.

Act (Accelerated Cognitive Therapy) targets six main processes to help a person manage their disorder. They are not followed religiously, but presented to the patient when necessary by the psychologist. These six processes are:

* Cognitive Defusion - This involves accepting your imagination or thoughts as they are and changing how you approach them to deal with them. ACT, which is based

on mindfulness-based therapy, doesn't tell you to skip a thought; rather, it encourages you to live it fully and approach it with an upbeat outlook. The goal here isn't to limit experiences but rather alter how you view a given situation.

* Accept - Recognize each thought as "just another thought," without giving it any weight. ACT helps individuals learn and practice ways of living through unpleasant or fearful thoughts without trying to escape them, eventually leading them to stop performing compulsions and move forward instead of struggling against them.

*Values - ACT utilizes a range of tools that enable individuals to identify the values most meaningful and precious to them. This helps them prioritize what needs to be prioritized in their life, making it clear what should take priority. Unlike other therapies, ACT does not instil values into people; rather, it helps them uncover existing ones, whether consciously or subconsciously.

* Self as Context - This is an intriguing step where ACT, through its various processes, helps people with OCD recognize that there exists a world outside their innermost experience. It encourages them to look beyond their personal struggles and understand that life is much more than our feelings, sensations, and thoughts; taking this step can make people significantly less afraid of their thoughts.

* Commitment or Committed Actions - Committing to action means taking one's values into consideration and working towards them through positive behaviors and practices. We must recognize how our behavior can shape us, so it is important that we maintain a positive outlook towards life and the environment.

* Connection with Present Time - Accepting that one cannot predict or change the future is key in dealing with anxiety about what might transpire in it. The only way to cope is to live in the present and embrace

every detail without trying to extrapolate anything from it.

ACT therapy does not focus on thoughts and the working of the mind, but rather how to manage them and utilize various approaches that can positively address intriguing notions. It does not involve exposure exercises but instead includes exercises that encourage patients to accept themselves and choose a path towards a meaningful life through conscious choices.

Why Opt for Acceptance and Commitment Therapy to Treat Obsessive Compulsive Disorder?

A study that has successfully proven the effectiveness of ACT therapy was conducted in 2006 by Twohig et al, who first treated subjects with this therapy before comparing results.

Following successful implementation of ACT therapy, reports revealed participants to be less motivated to engage in compulsive behaviors. They also experienced less urges to avoid or distract themselves from interesting thoughts and were less obsessive. Furthermore, after ACT was administered successfully, patients experienced decreased levels of anxiety or depression.

At present, ERP is considered the standard treatment for OCD; however, some patients may not respond to it at all. Therefore, alternative treatments like mindfulness-based therapy and Acceptance and Commitment Therapy (ACT) are increasingly necessary in order to meet patients' needs.

There is some circumstantial evidence to support these treatments for OCD (although most studies have been conducted on fewer subjects). Although these strategies require practice and dedication to be successful, once implemented they should significantly reduce urges to perform compulsions in patients.

Accepting Emotions

When feeling uneasy, the first step should be to exhale slowly and deeply while scanning your body from top to bottom.

You may experience unpleasant sensations by searching for the strong one - the one that annoys you most. This could be a lump in your throat, knot in your stomach, or pain in your chest.

Focus your attention on how it feels. Examine it curiously, as if you were an enthusiastic scientist exploring an intriguing phenomenon.

Be mindful of the sensation. Pay attention to its beginning and end points. Try to determine how far inside you it goes; where does the strongest sensation occur, followed by the weakest? Is the sensation pulsating or vibrating, light or heavy in nature, and what is its temperature?

Take a deeper breath and let go of any resistance you might be feeling towards that sensation. Breathe in slowly, creating space around it - don't try to like or desire it; just allow it to exist as is.

The idea here is to watch the sensation without thinking about it. When your mind starts commenting on what's happening, simply say "Thank you, mind" and return to observing. This could be challenging for some of you; if so, recognize it without giving in (recognition is like nodding your head in appreciation as if to say: "There you are. I see you.") Once acknowledged, return attention back to the sensation itself.

Do not attempt to suppress or alter the feeling. If it has changed itself, that's fine; if not, keep focused on it and allow yourself some space if need be. Focusing may take a few seconds or minutes before complete release - be patient; take all the time necessary - you are learning something special here!

Chapter 9: Additional Treatment Options

Other methods of treating various conditions.

OCD can be effectively treated through comprehensive treatments such as residential treatment programs or intensive outpatient programs that emphasize ERP therapy principles. Another potential treatment option for OCD may be deep brain stimulation (DBS), also known as DBS procedures.

Patients who no longer respond to traditional treatments may consider this alternative treatment approach. In this scenario, electrodes are implanted in the patient's brain in order to stimulate proper responses when given impulses. Another effective option for obsessive-compulsive disorder is TMS or transcranial magnetic stimulation (TMS).

This non-invasive treatment is commonly used for individuals over 22 and up to 68. It utilizes magnetic fields in order to stimulate nerve cells in the brain, while an electromagnetic coil is placed alongside their scalp near their forehead. Once stimulated, current electromagnets deliver a magnetic pulse which then activates those stimulated nerve cells back home.

At this point, we have examined several methods for treating obsessive-compulsive disorder. It is highly recommended to speak with a doctor promptly if one feels the need to take medications or receive any form of treatment. The most crucial thing is not to avoid OCD symptoms that might present themselves in someone.

Never neglect mental health and give it the attention it deserves; so that symptoms can be addressed early and the severity minimized. So, have a chat with your doctor as soon as possible and understand all necessary do's and don'ts in case you require any type of treatment.

Chapter 10: How To Maintain Success Long Term And Not Slip Backward?

Now that you have a thorough understanding of OCD and how it can be managed, let me offer some practical advice for maintaining recovery and avoiding relapse. Even if things appear to be going smoothly at present, OCD can suddenly flare up from anything and disrupt your daily schedule. Furthermore, anxiety is often to blame for initiating such episodes.

Once you acknowledge it, it can take an immense amount of effort and time to overcome. OCD is considered a lifelong condition and can be managed through therapy and medication; however, one effective way of keeping yourself on track and not letting yourself slip away is self-care - in this chapter I'll offer some tips for doing just that.

Eat Healthy Food

Eating healthily and regularly is key when it comes to your diet - not just one day of the week. Even if you decide that today will be your day for eating well, what about all other days in a week? Eating nutritious and balanced food each day and keeping it consistent are the only ways you'll reap its rewards. Eating well has been scientifically proven to support OCD recovery when done consistently over time. So make it part of your plan-

Protein - Eating protein helps enhance many neurotransmitters in your brain, such as Gamma-Aminobutyric acid (GABA). This neurotransmitter has been known to relax an overly stimulated mind, making it particularly helpful for OCD sufferers.

Serotonin, also known as the happy hormone, is an important neurotransmitter found in proteinaceous foods. Eating protein causes tryptophan to be released into your system which in turn releases serotonin (although some studies suggest

OCD patients have very small amounts of this neurotransmitter).

Protein intake also plays a role in controlling dopamine levels, as this compound is derived from phenylalanine (an amino acid). Many brain imbalances are connected to these three neurotransmitters and OCD is no exception.

Protein sources to consider include legumes, seeds, nuts, seafood, poultry, eggs and grass or organic meats. If you are vegan while recovering from OCD it is especially important to maintain an appropriate protein intake to keep your neurotransmitter levels stable.

Good Fats - Eating healthy fats is just as important for your overall wellbeing as protein. These can be found in seeds, nuts, olive oil and coconut oil; grass-fed animal meats; avocado; ghee; plus food items high in omega 3s such as salmon, sardines or mackerel; Chia seeds or flaxseed.

Do you ever stop to consider why carbohydrates are so beneficial for mental health? The answer lies within: 60% of the human brain is composed of fat! Your brain messages travel through neurons that rely on fats for proper development.

Fats have been known to enhance brain performance and make your mind sharper. Furthermore, healthy fats provide relief from inflammation due to their anti-inflammatory effects.

At the same time, it is essential to remember that while increasing the consumption of healthy fats, you should simultaneously decrease the intake of unhealthy trans-fats found in packaged foods and baked goods.

Fresh Fruits and Vegetables - Fresh produce should never be overlooked when it comes to nutrition, especially fresh fruits and vegetables. Not only are these essential for your body's wellbeing, but their micronutrient content makes them especially important in our diets.

Not only do fruits and vegetables aid in several essential chemical reactions throughout the day, but they also keep your brain healthy. To start, increase your magnesium, zinc, vitamin C and most importantly vitamin B intake - always opt for organically grown produce! Additionally, incorporate them into every meal you eat!

Another tip I can offer you is this: reduce or avoid caffeine-containing items such as coffee, tea and soda to reduce anxiety levels.

Avoid Your Fears

It is essential for OCD patients to not ignore their fears. Avoidance only serves to trigger more symptoms, and taking shortcuts around these feelings could cause more obsessive-compulsive thoughts to creep in. Therefore, the most common advice given for supporting recovery from OCD is that one should confront their anxieties head-on.

Expose yourself to triggers that might trigger you, and then work on delaying their onset. Even if this leads to performing the compulsion at first, don't feel compelled to fight it; simply reduce its frequency over time. With more exposure, triggers will become automatic for you and less anxious than before; ultimately giving you more overall control.

Another thing to keep in mind is that obsessive thoughts can come at any time. With this attitude, you won't feel caught off-guard when the thought occurs and can better utilize all the tools you've acquired through therapy sessions. But if you keep telling yourself these thoughts won't occur, then you will only end up confused and not knowing what steps to take next.

Risk is an inevitable part of life - even when recovering from OCD. No matter how hard you try, risk will always remain with you. Accept this and living a normal life while having OCD will become much simpler.

Some people try to comfort themselves or their families out of fear, but this should never be done. Instead, accept reality and tell yourself what lies ahead for you or has happened to you. Reassurance only serves to negate any positive effects therapy might be having on you and become an obstacle on the path towards improvement. Regardless of why it becomes habitual to seek assurance, at its core it's nothing more than another form of compulsion.

Even if you experience compulsive or obsessive thoughts from time to time, it is preferable not to argue or discuss them with yourself. Instead, accept those feelings as real and tell yourself they exist. Spending more time avoiding such thoughts only serves to further distance yourself from recovery; oftentimes avoidance has the opposite effect on OCD patients who begin thinking more intensely about these things.

Don't React in a Binary Way

As you recover from OCD, there may be times when you make an error - that's okay! No need to feel guilty or guilty about these instances. If the urge does arise to give in to compulsion, try something else so that the urge can't take hold. Remember: this journey is long-term and there will be many chances at redemption along the way.

Follow Your Prescriptions

It is essential to stay on track with your doctor's prescribed treatments in order to support your recovery and avoid falling behind. While it can be tempting to indulge in alcoholic beverages or drugs for a moment, remember that these triggers will ultimately have detrimental effects in the long run.

At first, taking that first sip of alcohol may seem to temporarily alleviate your anxiety - but only momentary. Medication and therapy are the only effective treatments for OCD; by the time all traces of it have gone from your system, more anxiety will return. Smoking cigarettes also has similar effects due to their nicotine content which acts in much the same way as alcohol does.

Be Patient with Your Progress

Good things take time; success does not happen overnight. Remember this when feeling impatient about your progress or that it appears to be moving too quickly for you. Everyone moves at their own pace, so just because someone else has made more progress than you doesn't guarantee the same level of success for yourself.

Stay confident and focused on one day at a time. Do all your therapist's suggested homework and finish what you have planned for that day. Create micro-objectives to achieve small wins over time - that way, you can see long-term progress.

One important tip to keep in mind is the necessity of reviewing your progress and tasks periodically. Even if you think that everything is clear in your head, it won't hurt to go over them again. Without regular review, the human mind can easily forget difficult tasks or neglected important items if left undone.

If you are having difficulties with an assignment for OCD patients, speak to your therapist about it. While all OCD patients must complete certain tasks each day, your therapist can continually modify these tasks according to your progress or current circumstances. But sometimes you may have been given a task which you do not wish to complete.

If this applies to you, make an appointment with your therapist and discuss the situation openly. Don't try and fix everything - that would only serve to exacerbate things. Remember: this is your own therapy, so you have every right to express any feelings or concerns that come up. Additionally, be vocal if something doesn't feel comfortable; otherwise, keep looking for solutions elsewhere.

The ultimate purpose of each task given by your therapist is to induce just enough anxiety that you can manage it comfortably. Your therapist never wants you to feel overwhelmed with an assignment or setback, and so it's important that you are open to pushing yourself a little farther with each task as this is how progress is made.

Some OCD patients take too long to begin their assignments. They assume the ideal moment is coming soon enough, but as the old saying goes: the perfect time to start is now! The more you try and plan a certain timeline for starting something, the greater the odds for procrastination - something

OCD sufferers often experience to a great degree.

So, to combat this issue, make it a habit of starting on your assignments the day they arrive - this way, you won't feel overwhelmed with them. Additionally, review each day's tasks before they're due so that even if you forget some details, your therapist won't notice.

Maintain a Journal

As you go through OCD treatment, there will be strategies that work great and others that don't seem to. To keep track of what works for you and what doesn't, keeping a journal is the best way to do so.

This will keep all your productive efforts in one place, so even if you experience particularly challenging days, you can always refer back to your journal and follow the strategies that have proven successful in the past.

Your journal doesn't have to be perfect; the primary objective should be capturing all the important points that have contributed to your recovery process. By recording these thoughts in writing, they will serve you in the future when feeling lost or uncertain about what helped you last time. Plus, keeping a journal also serves to remind yourself of all your accomplishments against OCD and instill confidence when feeling down.

When life gets challenging, your journal can be a great tool to focus on what makes life simpler and prevent compulsive thoughts from taking over. Your success story will continue to build over time, making you even more proud and secure in yourself.

One important thing to remember here is that success should always come before failure. Sometimes in life, you just need to sit back and appreciate yourself for doing something right and applying coping strategies correctly; doing so will motivate you further down the right path.

At first, you may not see the benefits of journaling immediately, but over time you will come to appreciate its power. It provides a tangible reminder of your progress in conquering OCD; this boosts self-esteem and confidence so that you are even more motivated to fight for recovery and maintain it.

Avoid Chasing Perfectionism

Perfectionism can be a real issue for OCD patients. But your focus should not be let it distract you. Your brain may tell you that in order to achieve recovery, you must get everything just right; otherwise, things won't go as planned and this means being perfect while completing task assignments. But this should never be your goal!

But does it really work this way? No! The more devoted you become to perfection, the higher the likelihood that compulsive behavior may develop as a pattern in your life.

How can you tell if you are striving for perfection? Watch out for signs that you are being too rigid in following rules and doing things the same way every time in an effort to reach a certain level of perfection.

One more thing I would like to emphasize is the importance of not dedicating your whole day solely to finishing a task. Remember that this should only be part of your life and not take over completely; make sure you also take time out for yourself and enjoy life as fully as possible.

But when trying to avoid perfectionism, don't give in to thoughts like 'it's only an assignment' and 'it doesn't matter in real life.' Your assignment is meant for your benefit - if you do it simply because your therapist told you too, then it won't work. You must do it voluntarily and understand everything completely as well.

When working on your assignment, pay close attention. Don't allow your mind to wander or disconnect for any reason - this will only hinder progress and ultimately result in negative outcomes. Your mind often attempts to disconnect itself out of anxiety; however, rather than trying to avoid it altogether, try dealing with the anxiety instead of trying to suppress it.

A great solution to combat anxiety is to focus solely on your assignment when it's due. Avoid engaging in other distracting activities at that time. Your anxiety needs to be managed, not run away from, so if you want that outcome, don't escape - stay present!

Do not back away from a challenge just because it seems difficult. Always view this as an opportunity for growth and remember that each new challenge offers another chance at mastery; so, embrace each opportunity as its own reward and keep practicing!

When working on your assignment, take your time. Don't rush into it to avoid feeling anxious. Try to view the task in a positive light that will help you improve. Your objective should not be to finish quickly but rather allow some moderate levels of anxiety into your mind so that you can build up tolerance towards them.

At the same time, if your assignment is going well and there's no indication of nervousness in you, inform your therapist. Give yourself at least a week or two to complete the assignment without any stress, then see if that continues - some tasks might not cause immediate anxiety but will eventually.

Chapter 11: Understanding Obsessive Compulsive Disorder And Its Symptoms

Obsessive compulsive disorder is an anxiety disorder that may present with various signs and symptoms.

Obsessive-compulsive disorder (OCD) is a mental health condition characterized by persistent thoughts, feelings or behaviors which are considered intrusive and undesirable. Obsessions and compulsions are terms used to denote these ideas and actions respectively.

Obsessions are persistent, repetitive thoughts, images or desires that cause significant distress or anxiety.

People suffering from OCD often recognize that these thoughts may be inappropriate or unreasonable, and often come to understand that they lack foundation in reality.

Obsessions may manifest as a need for symmetry or order, an obsession with injury or danger, or fear of contamination, among other signs.

Compulsions are behaviors or rituals that OCD sufferers engage in to alleviate the fear or distress caused by their obsessions.

Compulsions may involve excessive hand washing, checking, ordering or cleaning and may be ritualistic in nature. While compulsions are often performed to reduce anxiety or prevent an feared event from occurring, they are rarely enjoyable in themselves.

OCD symptoms can range in intensity and make it challenging to carry out everyday activities.

Here are some telltale signs of OCD:

Experience thoughts or emotions as persistently bothersome and unwelcome an excessive emphasis on symmetry, order or perfection excessive washing of hands or cleaning

Excessive monitoring or seeking assurance

An excessive need to carry out duties or perform procedures a certain way

Trouble letting go of things. Struggles making decisions.

Avoiding situations or things which cause compulsions or obsessions.

OCD is often a chronic illness that requires ongoing management to keep symptoms under control.

Cognitive-behavioral therapy, medicine, or a combination of the two may be employed as treatments.

With the right guidance and support, OCD sufferers can learn to manage their symptoms and enhance their quality of life.

Contrary to popular belief, Obsessive Compulsive Disorder (OCD) patients do not exhibit excessive neatness or have an affinity for patterns or straight lines.

Alexa, 28, a 28-year old working in medical research, examines the myth surrounding this devastating ailment and believes it's time to change this unsatisfying narrative.

On this Friday night, you look forward to enjoying a pleasant dinner party hosted by your friend. From the corner of your eye, you catch sight of the color-coded books arranged neatly in a row.

When discussing OCD with someone, they usually respond, "OMG I know right, I'm so OCD!" You may not even notice OCD if you don't live with it; but if you do, phrases like this can bring on intense feelings of anxiety and may even lead to negative effects during recovery.

Obsessive-Compulsive Disorder, commonly referred to as OCD, is an anxiety disorder.

OCD is often misunderstood and stigmatized. Therefore, OCD Awareness Week serves as the perfect opportunity to debunk some myths so we can all gain a better insight into this disorder as individuals, together.

"Every time someone says to me 'I'm so OCD'," the patient shared, "it makes me doubt my diagnosis and prevents me from starting therapy."

Obsession, which begins with the letter O, can be an intensely distressing experience when they arise from unwanted thoughts, images, urges or sensations that do not fit with the personality of the sufferer.

Obsessions can take on many forms and are always directed at the sufferer's most prized possessions. As anxiety disorders, their goal is to force you face your greatest fears in order to prevent them from occurring.

OCD will respond in exactly that way - every day and second. For instance, if you value kindness towards others more than anything else, then being a narcissist may be more worrying than being attacked with an axe.

It is true that you can obsess over virtually anything, from whether or not you are in an appropriate relationship to whether or not you are gay, a child molester, or HIV positive - even whether or not Shrek will transform into you! Nothing is off limits here.

Compulsions begin with the letter C and refer to any behavior, action, or thought a person engages in to stop or reduce the effects of their obsessions. Compulsion-based behavior may reinforce obsessions and weaken the effects of treatment strategies.

Compulsions may be visible, such as making sure the doors are locked, or unseen, such as repeating a prayer in your mind to block out an offensive thought.

Be Prepared for the Disorder.

Here, I will explain why it isn't considered "very OCD" to have your margins aligned on PowerPoint. Let's stop using OCD as an adjective or quirky trait - although, if you believe that keeping your house tidy and color-coding your spreadsheet indicate that you "are OCD", then feel free to continue on with this post.

Multiple characters in the media contribute to this misconception. OCD isn't the only disorder mislabeled; we've all heard phrases such as "I'm going psycho," "I'm so bipolar," and "That's so schizo" before.

It is simplistic to conflate OCD with other human emotions. If organizing one's home is considered a sign of OCD, I certainly don't believe it is. Additionally, never label yourself with a condition until you have received an official diagnosis.

Let's all stop using OCD as an adjective or peculiar trait.

OCD is an awful condition, yet those suffering from it wish it were unique and cute. Obsessions can control, devastate, or even lead to someone taking their own life. You are not diagnosed with OCD if you have a preference for something like keeping your house tidy (the word preference is essential here).

My illness does not appeal to me in any way.

Let's revisit that dinner gathering. Sometimes I get the urge to avoid being that person who disrupts the atmosphere by telling others what they may and may not say at a gathering.

But every time someone says, "I'm so OCD," it causes me to doubt my diagnosis and puts off starting therapy. So please, change the narrative and be that person!

Although everyone experiences OCD differently, it typically leads to a consistent pattern of thoughts and behaviors.

1. What constitutes OCD? OCD has three main components.

Obsessions are when an unpleasant, distressing idea, image or urge repeatedly enters your mind. This obsession often causes intense anxiety or other unpleasant emotions to accompany it.

Compulsions: Repetitive actions or thoughts an OCD sufferer feels compelled to perform due to fear and anguish caused by their obsession.

Fixations and anxieties eventually return, breaking the cycle; however, compulsive behavior only temporarily alleviates symptoms of tension.

Although OCD can manifest in either as compulsions or thoughts, most sufferers experience both.

At some point, most people experience unpleasant or unwanted thoughts such as the possibility of forgetting to lock the front door of their house or encountering unexpectedly insulting or violent mental imagery.

However, you may experience an obsession if a persistent, unpleasant thought occupies so much of your thoughts that it interferes with other ideas.

Obsessions that often plague those suffering from OCD include:

Fear of intentionally harming yourself or others, such as injuring children or other members of your family; a need for symmetry or orderliness (e.g., making sure all tin labels face in the same direction); and fear of accidentally harming yourself or others--like worrying that you might set the house ablaze by leaving the oven on accidentally--can all contribute to these fears.

You may experience disturbing or unpleasant obsessive thoughts of a violent or sexual nature. Remember, these are only thoughts, and simply having them does not require you to act upon them.

1.2 Obsessive Actions

Compulsions often begin as an attempt to lessen or prevent distress caused by an obsessive thought; however, these behaviors may either be excessive or have no real connection to the original thought.

Someone worried about getting sick may want to wash their hands repeatedly, while someone concerned about hurting their family might feel the urge to repeat something several times in an attempt to "neutralize" the concern.

Many OCD sufferers are aware that their behavior is unreasonable and illogical, yet they find it impossible to stop and believe they must continue doing it "just in case".

Common compulsive behaviors experienced by OCD sufferers include:

Cleaning, washing hands, checking to see if the gas is off or that doors are secured, ordering items to hoard, asking for assurance and considering "neutralizing" ideas to block out obsessive thoughts, avoiding locations or circumstances that might trigger obsessions are some of the steps they can take.

Obsessive-compulsive disorder (OCD) is a mental health issue where someone's repetitive thoughts and activities become overwhelming. OCD can significantly disrupt one's daily life, causing significant distress and disruption from these disruptive thoughts and actions.

Young adults may develop OCD for various reasons, including:

OCD often runs in families, suggesting that it may have an inherited cause.

Brain Chemistry: According to research, OCD may be caused by an imbalance of specific neurotransmitters such as serotonin in the brain.

Environment Factors: Traumatic or stressful life events or experiences, like abuse, may contribute to the development of OCD.

Developmental Concerns: According to some studies, OCD may be caused by problems with the growth of certain brain circuits.

Diseases: According to some studies, some individuals may develop OCD as a result of contracting specific infections like streptococcal.

It is essential to remember that the exact cause of OCD remains unknown and likely varies from individual to individual. Therefore, seeking medical help and speaking with a mental health expert for an accurate diagnosis and treatment plan are your best bet if you are experiencing OCD symptoms.

Chapter 12: Ocd Diagnosis And Evaluation

Obsessive-compulsive disorder (OCD), a mental health disorder, is characterized by obsessive thoughts and compulsive behaviors. This condition may be chronic and incapacitating, severely restricting one's day-to-day activities.

OCD symptoms often overlap with those of other mental health conditions, such as anxiety disorders or attention deficit hyperactivity disorder, making the diagnosis of OCD in young people (ADHD) challenging.

To guarantee the proper treatment is administered, obtaining an accurate and complete diagnosis is paramount.

Young adults suffering from OCD can be diagnosed and evaluated in several ways:

Physical examination and medical history: When diagnosing OCD, the first step should be to gain insight into the patient's physical and mental health histories.

As part of this process, it is important to inquire about any physical or mental health issues, medications, and family medical history. Additionally, a physical examination may be performed in order to rule out any underlying medical disorders that could be causing the symptoms.

Psychological Assessment: To ascertain a person's symptoms and determine if they meet the criteria for an OCD diagnosis, a mental health professional such as a psychologist or psychiatrist will conduct a psychological assessment.

In this instance, a systematic interview, techniques for standardizing assessments, and behavioral observations of the subject could be employed.

Differential Diagnosis: Before diagnosing OCD, it's essential to rule out any other disorders that could be causing the person's symptoms. Conditions like ADHD or anxiety disorders that share symptoms with OCD must also be excluded.

OCD Severity: OCD severity can differ drastically between individuals. When selecting a treatment plan, the patient's level of symptoms must be taken into consideration when making your selection.

Overall, a comprehensive assessment by a mental health expert is necessary to accurately diagnose and assess OCD in young people.

If you or someone close to you is showing signs of OCD, it's essential that they receive professional help.

OCD is a neuropsychiatric disorder that often manifests during childhood, affects 1-2% of the population, and significantly impairs functioning throughout life. A comprehensive, evidence-based assessment is the initial step in diagnosing and treating OCD.

This research explores the administration practicalities, psychometric characteristics and limitations of commonly utilized assessment tools for adults and children with OCD.

Diagnostic interviews, clinician-performed symptom severity ratings, self-report assessments and parent/child assessments form part of this process.

In addition, the discussion includes adjunct measures that assess key linked characteristics (like impairment, family accommodation and insight).

At the conclusion of this paper, we provide recommendations for an evidence-based assessment that are guided by individualized assessment goals such as making an OCD diagnosis, assessing symptoms severity and tracking treatment outcomes.

1. An Assessment of Obsessive-Compulsive Disorder Based on Evidence

Obsessive-compulsive disorder (OCD) is a neuropsychiatric condition that commonly impacts young children, affects between 1%-2% of the general population, and has significant detrimental effects on individuals across all ages.

This research examines the practicalities, psychometric characteristics, and limitations of commonly used assessment tools for adults and children with OCD.

Diagnostic interviews, clinician-performed symptom severity ratings, self-report assessments and parent/child assessments all form part of this evaluation process.

The discussion also includes adjunct measures that assess critical linked characteristics (like impairment, family accommodation and insight).

At the conclusion of this paper, the recommendations for an evidence-based assessment are based on individualized goals that include making an OCD diagnosis, assessing symptoms severity, and monitoring therapy effectiveness.

Assessment, evidence-based rating scales, symptoms severity and therapy for obsessive-compulsive disorder.

In both clinical and research settings, an exhaustive evidence-based assessment is essential for accurately diagnosing the presence and severity of obsessive-compulsive disorder (OCD).

Given that OCD symptoms often manifest internally and people with this disorder may not be inclined to recognize or report them, assessing its symptoms can be challenging (i.e., limited insight).

This paper summarizes commonly used OCD measures from research studies, to help clinicians more accurately diagnose and monitor symptoms during assessment and therapy.

First, a review of the psychometric qualities and practical application of measures is conducted. Starting with clinician-rated measures, then adult self-report measures, then finally adult symptom assessment tests are reviewed.

This paper first describes how to incorporate parent/child measures into an evidence-based OCD assessment (i.e., impairment, family accommodation and insight). Finally, it presents recommendations for conducting such an evidence-based assessment with unique goals and empirical support which conclude this paper's findings.

When creating an evidence-based assessment battery, several criteria should be taken into consideration. Prioritizing measures according to the assessment's main objective requires first recognizing them.

When screening for symptoms, measures with high diagnostic sensitivity might be given priority. Conversely, when faced with a differential diagnosis (such as differentiating OCD from anxiety disorder or depression), diagnostic specificity would take precedence.

Similar to this, priority should be given to assessment methods with established treatment sensitivity for monitoring changes in symptom severity during therapy.

Therefore, a pragmatic framework can assist in selecting measures to meet these objectives. Within this framework, physicians are guided by their understanding of which tool may be most practical, accurate and beneficial in any given circumstance.

Therefore, having access to an array of evidence-based assessment tools for OCD significantly enhances a provider's capacity to select the most accurate tool when diagnosing this illness and monitoring its progress throughout treatment.

This review used the following standards as a guideline for categorizing reliability and validity when describing the psychometric characteristics of tests included in it.

Psychometric evaluation of reliability relied on internal consistency, interrater reliability and test-retest reliability as the basis. Values >0.90 were considered excellent while values >0.80-0.89 had good reliability while those >0.70-0.79 had fair reliability and those below 0.70 had poor reliability. An intraclass correlation (ICC) value between 0.75-1.00 was considered excellent interrater reliability.

Good (0.60-0.74), reasonable (0.40-0.59) and poor (0.40) interrater reliability were indicated by lower ICC value ranges. A correlation of 0.80 was considered favorable for test-retest reliability, whereas values of

0.70-0.79 and 0.70 respectively indicated acceptable and unsatisfactory results. Convergent and discriminant validity were the foundations for psychometric evaluations of validity when making this determination.

A correlation value of >0.50 between the rating scale and other measures of obsessive-compulsive symptoms and severity was considered to indicate good convergent validity.

Correlation values between 0.30 to 0.49 and 0.10 to 0.29 indicated fair and poor convergent validity, respectively. Furthermore, correlations between the rating scale and measures of non obsessive-compulsive symptom severity showed good discriminant validity at 0.10-0.29.